WHAT Lies BEHIND THE CURTAIN?

Claire Gray

WHAT LIES BEHIND THE CURTAIN

ISBN 978-1-912009-24-4

Copyright © Claire Gray

First published 2019 by Compass-Publishing

Edited and typeset by The Book Refinery Ltd

www.thebookrefinery.com

The right of Claire Gray to be identified as the author of this work has been asserted in accordance with the Copyright, Designs and Patents Act, 1988.

A CIP catalogue record for this book is available from the British Library.
Printed and bound by CMP Ltd. Poole, Dorset.

This book is based on a true story.
To protect identities, all names have been changed in this book.
All conversations have been remembered and reproduced to the best of the author's ability.

In loving memory of Uncle Peter,
who passed away peacefully on 21st January 2019.

CONTENTS

'Those who have the most broken wings can learn to fly again.'

– Claire Gray

INTRODUCTION

'Who am I?' and 'Why am I here?' are questions I've asked myself when I've been standing at a crossroads and wondering which way to turn. It's from these quiet moments that there comes a point when we look deep within ourselves, start to fully connect with who we are and reflect on our personal journey so far. This forms a relationship with oneself, which will be the only constant, evolving relationship in anyone's life. By having an awareness of self, we'll be on the right road to knowing who we are in relation to one another.

In life, we travel along a road that we've either chosen or been coerced to choose, and what we've experienced has in some way shaped us and formed part of the person we are today, whether we like it or not. Some encounters will have had a positive or negative effect on the way we see ourselves and the outside world, and some experiences may have been too traumatic to express with spoken words.

We're here for a short time, and everyone will have a story to tell at the end of it. Some people who cross our paths may have similar narratives to us, but we'll only find this out if we take the time to open up and listen to them. However, there will be pages of our stories that we don't wish to read out loud and would love to erase because we don't want to be reminded of some of the difficult times we've lived through. I thought that, by burying some traumatic chapters in the darkest part of my mind, everyday life would be fine, but the skeletons in my closet came back to haunt me in later life.

I began writing my memoirs at age 27; this was the time

when I walked away from my first long-term relationship, which was wrapped in not being honest and true to who I was. Back then, I used another to shield myself from outside intruders and the isolation I was feeling inside, because my boyfriend looked like a person who wasn't to be crossed. As I stood alone, without anyone for protection, I could look within and find myself through writing. I found that pen and paper couldn't be judgemental when I started to unlock Pandora's box. This helped me to unravel a past that was overshadowed by the groomers who took my innocence when I was a vulnerable, impressionable teenager. This first draft of my memoirs lay dormant until I decided to return to the beginning again.

On revisiting these memoirs at age 41, I saw myself differently, because I'm a far cry from the person who was ashamed of a path that wasn't my fault. I had matured in my perceptions of life experiences, and so this second stab at writing had a more powerful and cathartic effect on my self-healing and self-analysis. I chose to lose myself in the murky depths of my mind to find some meaning in how I had found myself in the clutches of a paedophile.

I started to reach this place of clarity when I looked into the world of counselling seven years ago. I had no idea what I'd be letting myself in for, and I found myself sitting in awe while listening to people's journeys, which explained why they were sitting in a room full of complete strangers. Their stories touched my soul, and I admired the strength and courage they demonstrated by speaking so openly and eloquently about their lives and the traumas they had suffered. On hearing their bravery, I endeavoured to do the same.

When attending the training school each week, I could fully be myself and share some chapters of my life so as to find understanding in the crazy world we all find ourselves tangled up in. I had space to get answers to my questions, by looking at my early life through adult eyes, and I began to grieve for the lost innocence I suffered through rape. Being in a supportive and nurturing environment allowed me to work through the emotions attached to the trauma I'd been through. I no longer wanted to be that person holding onto blame, shame and guilt. I took hold of the lost adolescent child I left in the darkness of my mind, and gave her the forgiveness and compassion she deserved, since she was too young to understand the cunning and manipulative world of grooming.

By sharing parts of our story, we can begin to transform ourselves. If we can say, 'I can't change the past, but I can change the way I look at my future,' then we're halfway to living an authentic life and not allowing ourselves to be defined by something that happened earlier on in our lives. What counts is the way we deal with what has been dealt to us and how we let the experience shape our lives into the person we become. By reliving and unravelling unresolved issues, we can shed a dark past and gain a future that's bright.

This journey will begin with who I was when I found myself as a young teen with a promising modelling career ahead of me, yet completely unaware that I'd be groomed into sexual activity with the owners of the modelling agency. The ending will be who I've become through acceptance, growth and self-discovery.

Before I start my true story, you may be wondering why I'm divulging such a traumatic experience. I believe we're all here for a reason and sometimes our purpose in life is to turn a negative experience into something positive to share with the world. Although I first wrote my memoirs 14 years ago, my intent remains the same – to help and bring awareness to others. Since the inception of the 'Me Too' movement, I've felt a push of energy and have been inspired by the many women coming forward to share their sexual-assault experiences. This is a time of great change, and for women to stand up and be heard. By revealing my story, I'm able to teach you the key lessons I learnt, which were not acting on my intuition and using my voice.

My vision for this book is that it'll be used to prevent others falling into a groomer's trap. Plus, no matter what has happened to us, this book can bring hope in the face of adversity, and show we can eventually heal from old wounds. I want to make things clear, so that when you reach the end of my story you'll have an understanding and clarity about the journey I've taken you on.

To begin with, I'll highlight the phases of sexual grooming and the behaviours my abusers used, which are similar to those phases and behaviours suffered by those who have been through or are going through the same experience. I refer back to these phases in the reflections I've written at the end of each chapter; these reflections will help you to recognise how the perpetrator reels their victims into a web of control and how their targets' autonomy is gradually taken by the groomer manipulating their chosen ones into doing anything they want them to do. In my experience, it's difficult to see what is going on when you're in the middle of it.

The phases of sexual grooming

Most people with a sexual interest in children will act on these desires. If they have easy access to minors, they'll begin a grooming process to prepare the child for sexual encounters to occur. This process varies in terms of how long it takes – it can take months; however, in my case, it took years. Sex offenders have different preferences when it comes to the targets they choose. My offender preferred white females beginning puberty, because he could easily coerce them and watch them develop into womanhood.

Groomers follow similar patterns of behaviour: they gain access to a situation through which they can then select their victims (phase 1), befriend the child to build trust (phase 2), build dependence (phase 3), isolate them from their loved ones (phase 4), blur the boundaries (phase 5), desensitise the minor with touch before the eventual stage of violation through sexualising the relationship with the child (phase 6), and – finally – maintain control (phase 7).

The following is a summary of the seven grooming phases I experienced over a three-year period.

Phase 1

Grooming can happen to anyone, from any walk of life. However, some people are more susceptible to it than others – especially minors. While the majority of paedophiles are men, women can also be sexual abusers of minors too. Paedophiles are planners, and they find ways to prey on vulnerable young people who are insecure, gullible and emotionally needy. They can target children online, or they could be a teacher, coach, family member, friend or someone in the same-age peer group.

My sex offender used a modelling agency as a front to gain access to impressionable young girls. In this environment, he could target the victims who were the most desirable for grooming, to allow him to satisfy his sexual need to rape teenage virgins.

Phase 2

During this phase, a relationship is formed that prepares the minor for sexual abuse.

My abuser gradually built trust in his victims with the help of his girlfriend, who befriended aspiring young teenagers, then he gained the teenagers' respect by saying he was a valuable member of society because he was an ex-police officer. This encouraged me to let my guard down, which allowed him to gather information on my background and growing needs. My relationship with both my groomers was based on seeing them as mentors guiding me towards a future career. However, for him, it was a way of priming his prey with kind words to build a bond.

Also, predators are known to groom their targets' parents and lead them to believe that the groomer is beneficial to their child's life, so the parents become open to the abuser taking an interest in the child. Once the perpetrators have gained the parents' trust, they manipulate and mould the relationship to their advantage.

Phase 3

Most groomers are in no rush when it comes to the methodical process of grooming, as they need to make sure they have their victims' full trust. These relationships are made to look like healthy, positive relationships to the outside world.

Through this subtle behaviour, mine made me depend on him, by me working at the modelling agency, and him paying me a wage. This led to me spending more time in his presence and becoming emotionally reliant on both my groomers, as they took an added interest in my life.

Once my abuser had selected his models, he enticed us to stay at what he called the 'models' house'. This was a ploy to groom his favourites further, by spoiling us with dinners and drinks, which helped bond us as a group each week. In life, we're taught to believe that there's safety in numbers. However, this was part of his plan to make his grooming behaviour and any sexual encounters seem normal. We followed each other; it was like being in a cult.

Phase 4

Isolation begins when the relationship has been established. Offenders insert themselves more into the daily lives of their targets.

Gradually, I became isolated from my family and friends when my groomers took me to outside activities and let me stay at the models' house without the others sometimes. This reinforced my connection with them, which made me think I was special because I had been singled out.

Following this phase, they began to strip me of my autonomy by changing my name and taking control of my mind through brainwashing. This led to me being introduced to powerful businessmen and the high life, which was very seductive to a naive girl like me. Robert had a hidden agenda with his perverted, wealthy friends, which was to manipulate and take advantage of teenage beauties when they came of age.

Phase 5

The boundaries become blurred during this phase. Groomers start to desensitise their targets to inappropriate behaviours, which are not always physical.

Offenders prod and poke for intimate details about our lives. My abuser wanted to hear about any boyfriends I'd had and any sexual stories I could disclose.

Other behaviours that blurred the boundaries were his lounging in his underpants and flicking onto pornographic TV channels when we stayed at his home. However, through his comments regarding his behaviour, his actions were made to seem innocent. Following this, his girlfriend helped by beginning to desensitise me to touch by giving me cuddles, kisses and massages.

The use of alcohol was introduced at this stage, which makes you less inhibited to the groomer's (or groomers') hidden agenda.

Phase 6

Once the boundaries have been blurred, a violation is certain to follow. The special relationship becomes sexualised, and when this boundary is crossed there's no going back to life as it once was.

Because of the slow grooming process I experienced that led up to the abuse, I was unable to see my groomers for who they were. They exploited my vulnerabilities and stimulated feelings of curiosity about the sexual part of the relationship; for a teenager, exploring sexuality is a potent time. However, my abusers left me confused. I was at the awkward age of consent, where their advances towards me were intended to make me feel that I had wanted it all along, and so I had to engage in sexual activities. This sexual contact made me feel trapped, powerless and unable to control any situations with them. Later, this led to the main offender drugging and raping me.

Phase 7

The final stage of grooming is maintaining control. This is done through the dependence and emotional attachment formed. The victim thinks they cannot turn to anyone else for support, which leaves the groomer in a position of power and control. The perpetrator is always one step ahead and pays attention to the growing needs of the minor in front of them.

My abuser did everything he could to keep me close, so I wasn't able to leave. If an abuser thinks there's a threat to their control over the victim, they may become aggressive in their behaviour and may even become physically violent. The skilful manipulation of grooming leaves you feeling bewildered. I didn't understand that I was being groomed and abused, because the brainwashing was gradual. My freedom of choice was taken without me realising. This is where the adult abuser maintains control until something of a miracle happens that stops the sexual assaults from continuing.

Piecing together the Jigsaw

Before I take you on this journey, I wish to highlight the help section at the back of this book, which has been written for both current victims of abuse and/or parents who think their loved ones are suffering from it. The last section begins with the grooming models, which is a guide to help parents identify the model of grooming used on their child. In developing the conclusion, I've linked my story with the abusers' grooming behaviour and the revelations I've had throughout the book. These links are signs to look out for if you think you're a victim. I've also included information on warning signs for parents and/ or carers, the children who are most at risk and what parents can do to help prevent children from experiencing abuse. This is followed by a list of where you can access help and guidance, on pages 262–3.

1

BUDDING ADOLESCENCE

It was the beginning of the 1990s, and Manchester was known as 'Madchester' for its music and raves. I was too young – at age 13 – to be hitting the clubs, so I hit the streets of Longsight and Gorton, and hung out with my friends in parks and at market stalls. From time to time, we asked friendly adults to go into the shops to buy cigarettes and alcohol for us, so we could get tipsy and feel somewhat grown up. I was tall for my age and looked like a stick insect, being all skinny legs and arms. I had a perm because it was fashionable, and even if I did look like a poodle, at least I was following a trend of the times.

During my early years, I had pretty much been sheltered, and I felt lucky to be part of a large family. I was raised in a working-class environment; both my parents worked and gave us everything they possibly could. We were lucky enough to be taken abroad each year, and it was through this travelling that I gained itchy feet and dreamt of exploring the world to a greater degree once I left school. I shared my parents with three other siblings, and – being the third child – I grew up to do things my own way and became fiercely independent.

On becoming a teenager, with the associated physical and hormonal changes, I became aware of how attractive I was and that boys were showing much more of an interest in me. I began to explore these new changes, and found myself dating my first boyfriend; however, the whirlwind of young love ended when he met someone else. This experience started the path of discovering my sexuality and who I was in relation to others.

Like most teenagers, I wanted to explore my identity outside the family environment and go out with my friends on a daily basis. My mother was strict with curfews, and if I came in even five minutes late, I'd be grounded the following day. With these restrictions, I found myself hanging out with a new friend called Leanne most of the time; she joined my school in Year 9, and we became close friends. Her mother was less strict than mine, and allowed Leanne a lot of free rein, which, in turn, helped me stay out after hours when I had sleepovers. This gave me space to think when I felt frustrated by being confined to a small environment. At Leanne's, I could tune in to my growing self, outside the family circle of protection.

My head of year sent another new girl my way, for me to make her feel welcome. Gemma was a pretty blonde, and was very much into her make-up and hairstyles. She was more outgoing and daring than Leanne and I were, and the boys loved her. Most weekends, we hit the city centre, shopping for clothes and make-up, and sometimes we would steal a lip gloss here and there from The Body Shop. I knew this was wrong and that if my mother found out, she would ground me indefinitely, but egging each other on gave us a buzz of naughty excitement.

Leanne always had the most money of the three of us, and this spurred me on to think of ways to earn my own. I knew if I wanted anything in life, I needed to get a job. I'd do any housework at home, which my father paid me for. And I was grateful for the extra money I gained when Leanne's stepfather gave us a job of sewing fabric onto mattresses, which were then sold on.

We hung out at Leanne's house most of the time, because it was usually free of adults. We typically stayed up late and tested make-up on each other, then compared ourselves as we gazed into the mirror at our transformations. I was struck by how much prettier I looked with make-up on, even if it was caked on. My father told me that I didn't need to wear it, but this didn't deter me from wanting to experiment. At home, I'd search through my elder sister's make-up bag and my mother's, if I could get hold of it.

When the house was quiet, I found myself looking deep into the mirror and asking questions such as 'Who am I?', 'Why am I here?' and 'Who will I become?' I felt lost sometimes, and desired to find a place where I belonged; I was searching for something, but I didn't know what. It was at this time that my life was to take a different direction, leading me into a world of deceit and manipulation, and my adolescent development was disturbed.

***

'I've found it!' Leanne squealed one evening when we were at her house.

I was draped over the couch watching TV, and I'd noticed Leanne searching through some paperwork and wondered what the hell she was doing. 'Found what?' I asked, turning to look at her in the hope of getting an answer as to why she was making all that noise.

'I went to a modelling agency last year; they taught us how to do our hair and make-up, and how to walk on the catwalk,' Leanne replied as she stood waving a phonebook in her hand.

My eye's widened.

'I joined for a while, but I left because I was going by myself.'

Leanne searched my face before continuing, 'Shall we go together? We'd have something to do every weekend.'

I sat up – after listening to Leanne rambling on – and I wasn't sure what to make of it all, but it sounded exciting, and so I went along with her enthusiasm.

'We could become professional models, and be in magazines, in catalogues, on the TV and do catwalk shows,' she added excitedly.

Leanne was so excited that she could barely contain it by the time her mother returned from work. I was fond of Leanne's mum, Barbara; she was kind and treated me like her own daughter. Leanne was always asking for things, and – because she was an only child – nine times out of ten, she would get what she wanted. I envied this at times, because I was the third child and had to put up with the dynamics of the family hierarchy, fighting for extra attention and affection, and trying to be heard over the others. Sometimes, I felt forsaken with respect to my growing needs in adolescence, but accepted this as my fate from having to share my parents.

'Mum, may I go back to the modelling classes? We're going to ask Claire's parents, and if they say yes, we can go together. I know I went last year and left, but now I won't be lonely if Claire comes along,' said Leanne, who then waited for her mother's response.

However, Barbara didn't really have a choice because Leanne had pretty much made her mind up and was going regardless of whether her mum agreed.

'Yes, you may; it'll be nice for you to go together. I'll give the modelling agency a call when Claire has asked her mum,' stated Barbara.

Leanne leapt up, kissed Barbara and almost kicked me out of the house.

'Ask your mum and then call me straight away!' said Leanne as she hugged me goodbye, opened the front door, ushered me out and closed the front door.

After leaving her house, I walked from her street towards a mossy field with a path that led me from Gorton into Longsight, which I then took. Walking this way home gave me the frights when it turned dusk, and so I always looked behind me, thinking someone was going to jump out and attack me. My gran's prayers would ring through my ears as my legs picked up speed, and I'd say to myself, 'Please, God, don't let anything happen to me; keep me safe.' When I approached the end of the field after walking across it, I breathed a sigh of relief. I felt safer when I stepped onto the streets of Longsight.

Continuing on my journey home, and turning into familiar roads and cobbled entries, I found myself lost in a fantasy, musing and picturing myself as a professional model. How adventurous that would be: dressing up, walking on the catwalk and being on the front cover of glossy magazines.

I walked dreamily into my house, which was always full of life, with the TV on, music playing in the background, and the sound of the conversations my parents and siblings were having. I headed to the kitchen, where Mum was preparing dinner. Sometimes, I found it hard to approach her about things and hated to interrupt while she was busy, but this couldn't wait.

'Mum,' I said cautiously, intending to test the water regarding her mood by the tone of her voice when she responded.

'Yes, what is it, Claire?' Mum asked.

Result, I thought, *she's in a good mood*. I continued, 'Leanne wants me to start modelling classes with her.'

Mum turned her attention to me.

'In the classes, we're taught how to do hair and make-up, and how to walk on the catwalk. They take place every weekend, so they won't interfere with school,' I explained. I waited at the kitchen door for a response.

'Whereabouts is the modelling agency and what's it called?' Mum queried, peeling potato skins onto newspaper.

'In town; it's called Northern Teen Models,' I said smiling brightly.

'Where did Leanne get this idea from?' Mum asked curiously.

'Leanne went last year, but stopped going because she had no one to go with. I'll need some money for the bus and a couple of quid for the class, if they take us on,' I replied.

Mum didn't seem convinced, but told me she would ring Barbara later that evening and would then wait until my father returned home from work before making a decision.

***

To my delight, my parents agreed; the only issue was that they couldn't attend the interview, but were happy for Barbara to accompany Leanne and me to sit through the discussion of what the modelling agency had to offer.

***

The next few days were a whirlwind of making things happen. No sooner had Barbara called the Northern Teen Models for an interview date than we found ourselves arriving at the building the following week; the autumn of 1990.

Leanne and I stood, with a feeling of nervous excitement, before two red doors.

'Here we are, Claire; this is where we can become models!' Leanne delighted in saying.

I was lost for words momentarily, facing the steps to take me into unknown territory. We walked in.

'OK, Leanne, let's stay calm and take a breath. We don't want to be getting ahead of ourselves,' Barbara said, fussing with Leanne's clothes, before leading us through another set of doors.

Standing in the small, dark hallway, I breathed in the smell of a musty, old building and looked up to a narrow staircase. The security camera in the corner caught my eye, which gave me the creeps because I was sure someone was watching us. The sound of us walking up some creaky steps was eerie; as we followed Barbara to the fourth floor, it seemed like we were in a haunted house rather than an office building.

We were slightly out of breath when we reached the top. Barbara had to use the banister to pull herself up from the last step, and she let out a sigh of relief. I chuckled as we stood for a moment, each catching our breath, before turning left into a small hallway and walking towards reception. I grinned while looking down the gated lift shaft and wondered why we hadn't used the lift. Through the glass window, a pretty young brunette stood up from her office desk to greet us at the reception door.

'Hello, I'm Barbara, and these are Leanne and Claire. We have an interview at 12pm,' Barbara said confidently.

I was hit by my reflection in the mirror on the right, and quickly adjusted some flyaway hair and placed it round my ears.

'Hi, I'm Cassandra; please come in,' said the girl in reception, and she pointed us towards some chairs.

Music played, and the faint sound of voices came from a room facing us, which had a little glass window in the middle of the door. My eyes flickered, spotting some girls walking about. The pigeon holes against the wall caught my attention next; these were where they stowed models' composite cards.

I daydreamed, imagining having a card showing professional shots taken of me. Cassandra broke my reverie, and I was instantly brought back to the room from my brief fantasy.

'I'll get you some forms to fill in. Please take a seat,' said Cassandra.

Our eyes followed her as we sat down.

Cassandra quickly grabbed some papers that were being blown by the breeze coming from the open sash windows. 'Here, please fill in these forms. Gina will be out shortly to explain how the modelling agency works, then you'll see Robert, the manager.' Cassandra squeezed herself between the two office tables to sit back at her desk.

I was a little anxious when I filled out the form and added my parents details without their presence, yet I felt grown up doing something so important without their guidance. (I had no idea this was going to be a significant turning point, and an experience that was to have a profound impact on my life in more ways than I imagined.) I attached a snapshot of myself to the form and sat patiently waiting to be called for the interview.

An attractive, slim woman, with large, hazel eyes and thick, luscious, mousy-coloured hair emerged from a room on the left. 'Hello, I'm Gina; it's lovely to meet you,' she declared, then gestured that we were to enter her office.

'Hi,' Barbara and Leanne said cheerfully, in sync.

'Hello,' I added and followed Barbara to a seat in the small, cosy room. I watched Gina step to the upper surface and push herself round the table to sit in front of us. I felt a little intimidated as I looked up at her from my chair.

Gina explained, 'I'm one of the bookers here at Northern Teen Models, and I'll tell you a bit about us and how we work.' Gina observed us; she certainly had our attention.

'Our motto is "We're here to work as a team",' she said proudly, before carrying on, 'We'll teach you how to become professional models. I've been with the modelling agency for over 10 years and have modelled from the age of 17.' Gina passed over her portfolio for us to look at.

We flicked through it, and I glanced at her because she looked different in the pictures.

Gina responded by saying, 'This could be either one of you in the future.'

Leanne and I turned to each other, bright-eyed; this comment was so seductive to 13-year-olds.

'These are lovely photos,' Barbara commented.

Gina passed us more portfolios of the professional models representing them. I was already spellbound by her words and with the books I held in my hands.

'If you join our team of models, you'll begin by attending the classes at the weekend. Which day was it you preferred?' Gina looked at our forms.

'Sundays,' we replied quickly, wanting her to continue.

'In the classes, you'll learn how to do hair and make-up, but mainly how to present yourselves and walk on the catwalk. You'll be required to wear a bathing suit for the classes, and some weeks we'll weigh you to keep an eye on your weight.' Gina paused for a moment. 'When we think you've progressed, and you've decided this is something you want to do, you'll have photographs taken so we can begin to promote you as professional models, and you'll go to castings to meet our photographers and clients for work.'

I was amazed how Gina said this so fluently. She looked down from her table to where we were sitting captivated while listening to her. It all seemed so real now. She had made such a big impression by planting a seed of what we could achieve in the future.

'Do you have any questions?' Gina asked and waited for a response.

I looked at Barbara for guidance because I was lost for words.

'No, I don't think so,' Barbara said, smiling.

'OK,' stated Gina, 'I'll see if Robert is ready for you now.' She left the room with our interview forms, leaving the door to slowly close behind her.

Leanne turned to face Barbara and looked innocently into her eyes, saying, 'Oh, I hope they say yes, Mum.'

'Yes, me too,' I quickly added. Never before had I wanted something so much in my life as I sat there eagerly waiting for Gina's return. Everything she said and all the books I saw that day had inspired me to want the same. I was a girl on a mission to succeed and nothing was going to stand in my way.

'I'm sure they'll take you on. They said yes last time, so I don't see any reason why they should say no now.' Barbara looked lovingly at us.

Gina returned and asked us to wait in reception for Robert; her eyes twinkled before she entered her office and closed the door.

We sat in silence, listening to the music and the faint sound of heels hitting the floor in the next room.

An office door swung open, which made my stomach flutter. A short, stocky man with dark hair, a beard and a beaming smile walked towards us. We stayed in our chairs and waited for his cue.

'Hello, I'm Robert. It's lovely to meet you all. Come and follow me,' he said cheerfully.

I studied his back as he casually walked ahead of us. He wore jeans and a polo shirt. Robert didn't quite fit what I had imagined the manager of a modelling agency to be like. I worked out that he could be in his 50s, because of the speckles of grey hair in his beard. I caught a glimpse of myself in the mirror again, and thought I looked OK in my jeans and bodysuit, and I was glad I hadn't put a tracksuit on.

Entering his room, I noticed how messy it was compared to reception, which was immaculate. Robert motioned for us to sit on the cream couch to the right of his door. Like the other rooms, it had a higher surface on which a grey desk sat in front of sash windows. He brushed past a closed, long, heavy-looking curtain to reach his seat. I was curious and thought, *I wonder what lies behind the curtain?* It appeared odd and out of place. It was like having a shower curtain as a door, because it seemed to lead to another room.

My eyes turned towards Robert as we sat waiting for him to say something. He scanned our interview forms and pictures before looking over his glasses, surveying me and then Leanne. Him peering down at us gave an impression of his superiority, and the glint in his eyes gave me the creeps as his glare was fixed upon me. My stomach flipped.

'Do your parents know you're here, Claire?' he said, staring intently into my face.

I hesitated, then replied, 'Yes, they know I'm here.' I could hear my voice quaking.

'That's good; I wouldn't want you starting the classes without your parents' consent,' he confirmed.

I breathed out inconspicuously, because I thought he might have said no.

'I think you're right for us and I'm pleased to say you can

both start the Sunday classes from 1–3pm next week.' He smiled wickedly and pushed our interview forms to the side.

'Oh, that's great news,' Barbara said delightedly, before looking down at us.

Leanne and I grinned at each other as we sat squished together; we seemed to have sunk into his couch, and I felt quite small sitting there.

'You'll need to bring your bathing suit, heeled shoes and £2 for the class,' he added, standing up.

Robert looked much taller standing on his platform, which made me feel even smaller.

'Come with me, and I'll show you what to expect next week,' he said as he stepped down to meet us and brushed past the curtain again.

I willed my eyes to peer in and take a look, but the curtain quickly draped back to its natural hanging place. (My curiosity was to be satisfied years later and not with what I innocently imagined lay behind it.)

Robert smiled, leading us out of his office and to the door with the little glass window; he peered in before opening the door. The music drummed louder in my ears, and he beckoned for us to peek in. Girls walked to the music, and I noticed the different styles of swimsuit each girl wore, realising suddenly that I didn't own a nice one. Mine were sporty and well used from the swimming I did each week. My mind ticked over, wondering how I could get my hands on a decent bathing suit.

'This will be you two in a few weeks,' Robert said, closing the door and leading us from reception. 'Goodbye, and see you next week.' He grinned – showing his perfect, white teeth – and pressed the button for the lift.

'Thank you very much,' Barbara replied.

Leanne and I smiled as we got in the lift and stood in the small space, followed by Barbara.

Robert closed one gate, and Barbara slammed the other shut. He nodded, and the lift jumped slightly, making a funny noise before descending. We watched his body disappear from sight and hugged each other excitedly at the thought of our destiny beginning to be mapped out before us.

***

Later, as I walked home from Leanne's, I had a spring in my step. I was feeling joyful that I would be able to call myself a model one day. I entered my house, full of life, and gushing about the modelling agency and what it had to offer. 'I'll start next week, in the Sunday class from 1–3pm, and I'll learn how to become a model and walk on the catwalk,' I told my parents enthusiastically.

'That's good, and you and Leanne will go together?' Mum interjected.

'Yes, I can't wait,' I confirmed. 'I could be in magazines one day.' With that, I ran upstairs to search my sister's drawers for a swimsuit to wear for my first day. I picked out a light-pink bathing suit and quickly stuffed it into my bag so she wouldn't notice.

Even though my parents were strict, they gave me a lot of freedom when they knew where I was. Being a typical teenager, I had a strong desire to step out into the world with an increased independence, away from my parents. I was developing a greater interest in peer relationships, and I was relying on those friendships for emotional support and on new people to confide in about physical changes. I was searching for a sense of belonging and seeking acceptance to fit in somewhere in the adult world. I wasn't sure what lay ahead, but I was eager to step into unknown territory, because this new path was much more inviting and exciting than the one I had been on.

However, unbeknown to me, the modelling agency was just a cover to the seedy world that lay behind it. I was going to be led along a road away from normal growth, following a paedophile and not knowing his full intentions. Through this experience, I'd transform into a young adult influenced by a background of grooming.

Reflections

The introduction to grooming starts when the adult abuser has some type of access to children. My groomer used Northern Teen Models as a front for procuring young girls for the benefit of himself and his circle of friends. I was in the early stages of adolescence, which is a crucial time in developing one's identity and building on the personality that was shaped in childhood. We start to form into the person we're about to become, as we leave our childhood behind and begin a new phase of adapting to adulthood.

The time when you are becoming a teen is when you are at a powerfully impressionable age, and is a time when your parents step back and allow you, the budding adolescent, more freedom to make choices. For an offender who is interested in young teenagers, this is a perfect age (if they have easy access to minors) to begin the grooming process. My abuser selected 'pretty girls', which is one typical characteristic of offenders in their search for prey.

For a young teen, the modelling agency was an exciting social outlet outside home and school life; however, the excitement overshadowed my voicing my curiosity about the curtain and the glint in his eyes. These were early intuitions, and everyone should trust and act upon these as you experience them, even if you're seduced with words about a bright future. In noting or writing intuitions down, you'll begin to see patterns unfold with the molester's behaviour. Groomers do not just jump into abuse; grooming is a gradual, organised and intentional process of manipulation.

On reflection, if I could give my 13-year-old self some guidance, I'd suggest questioning my curiosity and talking to a safe person. Our inner voice has meaning and talks to us all the time, and this instinct can serve to get us out of tricky situations that may become harmful in the future.

2
ON A PATH OF NO RETURN

The eagerly awaited Sunday arrived, and Leanne knocked on my front door.

'Are you ready?' Leanne asked with a grin as I greeted her.

'Yes, just a minute; I need to ask for some money,' I replied, opening the door wider to let her in.

Leanne came in and stood politely at the dining-room table while I approached the kitchen to find my father.

'Dad, may I have £2 for the modelling class and some bus fare, please?' I looked wide-eyed and innocently into my father's face.

'Yes, where's my wallet? Hi Leanne, I didn't see you standing there,' he said walking to the mantlepiece for some change.

'Hiya,' Leanne replied cheerfully.

'Thanks, Dad,' I said, taking the money, and I happily pecked him on the cheek.

'Have a good time and take care going into town. What time will you be in?' he asked.

My father's smile warmed my heart; he was a kind-hearted, caring man. I knew I could go to him anytime and ask for what I needed.

'I should be back before 4pm,' I replied.

'OK, dinner will be on the table by 5.30pm,' my dad confirmed.

I watched as he made his way back to the kitchen. I called after him, 'See ya later, Dad,' then I picked up my bag and left, with the door slamming behind me.

I always listened to my father. I was streetwise in many ways and this was down to the area I grew up in. However, the streets didn't seem as safe as they once did. At times, I had to watch my back for any gangs that tried to give me and my friends grief. I hated bullies and the jealousy from the members of girl gangs who wanted to fight you if you gave them the wrong look. I was unsettled that my neighbourhood was becoming unpredictable, with these types of people using force and intimidating others into taking something off you that took their fancy. More and more, I had to be one step ahead of the game and have my wits about me, so I wouldn't find myself in situations I couldn't get out of. I had witnessed some of my friends being bullied into having their jewellery taken away; however, I'd managed to evade the same fate, and removed my jewellery and placed it inside my pockets before they saw it. This uncertainty in my neighbourhood was driving me away from it and in another direction that felt safer, or so I thought.

***

Leanne and I arrived 20 minutes early for our first day at Northern Teen Models, and we took the lift to the fourth floor. I followed Leanne out of the lift and into reception, and we approached the office table hesitantly.

A young woman sat smiling at us. 'Hello girls, come over. I don't bite,' she said brightly. 'What are your names and ages?' she asked. Her blue eyes sparkled as she waited for an answer.

'Hi, I'm Claire, Claire Gray, and I'm 13,' I replied, feeling a little intimidated by this beautiful blonde's confidence, as 13 sounded so young. However, other names on the list had similar ages next to them, the youngest being 12.

'Hi, I'm Leanne and I'm 13 too,' Leanne added, sounding more self-assured than I did.

'That's £2 each, please,' said the blonde, 'Cassandra, will you show the new girls where to get changed?'

Turning round, I was relieved to see a familiar face from the interview process. Cassandra walked away, and we followed her past the queue of girls that had started to form behind us. I was amused by the way we all looked each other up and down on passing by.

Cassandra led us into the catwalk room. It was much bigger than I imagined it to be – we had only caught a glimpse of it the previous week. Chairs were placed against the back walls, and girls were sitting or standing talking to one another. The faint sound of music played in the background, which came from the curved table in the top corner of the room. Behind it, on the left, was a glass door that opened to the main reception. The noise of cars and buses from the main street intruded loudly through the open windows. Cassandra led us towards the end of the room. The whole back wall was covered with mirrors, and there was a mirrored door that she opened.

'Here, this is where you'll get changed each week,' she said. 'Put your bathing suits and heels on, then come out and take a seat when you're ready.' Cassandra smiled and left us to find a space in the narrow room.

More girls entered, giggling in conversation, and swiftly took their clothes off. I felt self-conscious undressing and stepping into my sister's costume; the other girls half-naked bodies distracted me as I glanced along the mirrored wall. I compared my body to theirs, and envied some of their large breasts and curved bodies; I wasn't full in that department and looked like a bean pole. I hoped my body would change and be more like theirs at some point.

When Leanne and I had finished fussing with our bathing suits, we walked tentatively into the catwalk room, which was now full of girls. We found seats in the corner and waited for the class to begin. The beautiful blonde from reception opened the glass door, came into the room, sat down at the desk and turned the music down.

'Hello everyone,' she said, 'We have a few new girls starting today. I'd like to welcome you to Northern Teen Models. I'm Shelly and I take the classes most weekends.'

Everyone's eyes were fixed on her.

She continued, 'OK, let's start with all of you walking one at a time, but not you new girls. Just sit and watch for now; you'll be taken to learn some basic steps later.' Shelly turned on the music for the class to begin.

I was even more nervous with the knowledge that I'd have to get up and do that one day. 'Shit,' I said, under my breath so Leanne could hear. 'What have you got me into?' I muttered, shaking my head.

Leanne turned and grinned at me. I watched each girl walk up and down the room, self-assured, and doing turns before sitting down.

'That was great, ladies; it was some good walking. Now, I'd like four girls up for the walk for eight [a type of catwalk routine], please.' Shelly turned the music up and stood at the top of the room, waiting for any girls to join her.

I scanned the room, and some girls from the top corner jumped up; these seemed to be the most popular girls in the class. I had noticed them when I first walked in. They wore trendy, girly clothes, and their hair and make-up was immaculate; I couldn't help comparing myself to them. I dressed like a tomboy most of the time, hardly wore make-up, and felt most comfortable in my shell suits and t-shirts, with my hair scraped off my face in a ponytail. I was engrossed in the moment, watching them do a routine to the music, and wished to be part of the cool group one day.

Gina disturbed the class when she entered the room; everyone looked up and smiled. Shelly turned the music off, and Gina asked, 'Will the new girls come with me, please?' Gina opened the door wider, and we stood meekly to follow her into reception. We huddled together, standing in the office like naughty school girls, wondering what to expect.

Gina soon explained, 'OK, I'm going to show you some half and full turns to use when you begin to walk on the catwalk. Please stand in a line and then follow what I do.'

We separated, and Gina stood in front of us and talked us through the first steps. We looked like stiff robots doing the same thing over and over again before we relaxed and went with the flow. This was the moment I started to see a glimmer of hope for my future, and I was determined to follow the dream that was beginning to build in my mind.

'Stand straight, with your shoulders back, and make a T shape with your feet; always be sure to start with your right foot,' instructed Gina.

I loved Gina's patience with us, and watched her help a girl position her feet correctly. I was surprised that I picked up the steps straight away. I felt at ease in Gina's presence, and I decided she would be my role model from now on. I was content to sit back in class until it ended.

However, this contentment turned into terror when Shelly said, 'Let's have the new girls at the top of the room, please.'

I was sure I hadn't heard right, as she couldn't be asking us to get up on the first day.

Shelly grinned; she could see how uncomfortable we must have looked trying to hide behind one another. 'All I want you to do is walk to the bottom of the room together, make a half turn at the top, then walk back.' Shelly said this like it was the easiest thing to do.

She waved for us to stand, and we gathered, huddling together again at the top of the room. Shelly turned the music up, and my chest started to thump as she counted us in to the beat of the music. My heart raced faster on reaching the bottom of the room; a few of the girls turned in the opposite direction to the rest of us. Walking back, I was sure some of the girls were sniggering at us, but not in a malicious way; it was more as if to say, 'We've been there too.'

'See, it wasn't that bad, was it? Well done, girls,' Shelly said and pointed us to our seats. The pitter-patter of heels filled the room as we went to sit down, and I allowed a sense of achievement wash over me.

'Let's finish with the walk for eight, for those who haven't done it today, then its home time,' Shelly added.

***

Leanne and I left the modelling agency in high spirits, and we travelled home chit-chatting about some of the girls in the class, before parting and going our separate ways. I felt my confidence had grown a little bit and I entered my parents' house full of life. I excitedly told my parents about my first day, and they listened as I rambled on. I now had something to focus on each week, as the classes gave me a sense of purpose, and those first two hours spent there were the start of many more to come, as the weeks turned into months and the months turned into years.

***

A few weeks later, having found my feet and being more settled, I began chatting with other girls before the class started. As always, when Shelly entered the room, the chatter faded, and we would sit respectfully waiting to follow her lead.

'Today, those of you who started a few weeks ago will get up on your own when we go round the room; you don't need to do many turns if you don't feel confident,' Shelly explained, as she surveyed the room.

I tried to sink into my chair and hide myself, but it didn't work.

'And that includes you, Claire Gray; I can see you hiding in the corner,' Shelly said with a grin.

I sat there, wanting the floor to swallow me up. *Those damn mirrors*, I thought, *There's no getting away from them.*

As my turn loomed, my heart beat faster and the palms of my hands began to sweat from anticipation. I tried to gulp down my nerves when the girl next to me confidently stood for her turn; this didn't help my anxiety. How I wished it was Leanne's turn first. After the girl sat down, I gritted my teeth in a smile and looked at Shelly. On her nod, I abruptly stood and positioned my foot in the T position to begin walking. It was a relief that I had an easy song to walk to – Shelly had great taste in music. I tapped my foot and waited for the right beat before I took my first stride. It seemed like everyone's eyes were piercing through my body, which made me feel exposed to the core, now that I was on display. I looked towards the popular girls and smiled, and – to my surprise – they smiled back, which reassured me I was doing OK. The adrenalin in my body pumped as I returned to my seat. I was thankful to sit down and to have finally got up on my own without the protection of the others by my side. It took a while for my heart to stop racing, and I hoped that this walking under the scrutiny of others would be easier as time went on.

Halfway through the class, Robert distracted me by peering through the window in the door; I quickly looked away, embarrassed because he had spotted me.

Sometime later, Gina walked in with a list of girls she was about to weigh. She had such a presence about her that everyone would stop what they were doing and admire her from head to toe. Every week since starting to attend the classes, I had watched girls go in and out of the changing room to be weighed by Gina, and this week – for the first time – Leanne and I found ourselves on the list.

'Claire Gray,' Gina shouted over the music.

I walked over coyly and stood next to her, waiting for Leanne to come out of the room, having just been weighed. Leanne and I smiled as she brushed past me, and I entered the room with Gina following behind.

'Take off your shoes and bathing suit, put the towel round you, and then knock on the door, and I'll come in and weigh you,' Gina said gently. I watched her leave the room, and I noted that I must start wearing the odd dress or skirt when I went to the modelling agency; my comfy tracksuits didn't seem to fit the dress code for a budding model.

I glanced round the empty room; it had a different atmosphere without the girls getting ready for the class. Being alone, I got a proper look round. I peeked out of one of the six arched windows to the back alley below, which looked a little creepy because the building opposite caused dark shadows in the room. I saw the scales in the corner and the blue towel draped over the chair, and realised suddenly that I might be taking too long. I removed my shoes and costume quickly, and picked up the towel, which was much heavier than what I'd taken off. I was puzzled by this and felt a little strange pulling the towel round my naked body. I walked towards the door, having a full view of the filing cabinet and the boxes filled with models' composite cards beside it. On the other side of these was a folded massage table. I peered at the black-and-white cards in one of the boxes before looking higher into an air grill, which had bigger gaps than normal; it seemed to stare at me. I hastily tapped on the door, and Gina came in smiling, which relaxed me. I followed her to the scales and stood on them, looking down. We waited for the noisy dial to make its final stop. Gina tugged the back of the towel slightly pulling it up then down from the small of my back, I looked at her curiously.

'I'm just checking you didn't leave anything on,' Gina explained. She looked down and wrote my weight on her list.

I waited for her to leave the room before I released the heavy towel from my body. I glanced at the air grill again, and it struck me that it was next to Robert's office. I felt nervous in my nakedness, as I caught sight of my slim, bare frame in the mirror. I quickly dressed and left the room. (The air grill never crossed my mind again until a few years later.)

***

Before the end of the year, when I had been attending Northern Teen Models for nearly four months, the head booker of the modelling agency made a brief appearance at the Sunday classes.

Shelly was proud to introduce us to Elaine, who was a tall, slim brunette with grey eyes. She sat in on the class, and everyone was eager to make a good impression. However, her watchful eyes made me self-conscious. We were split into groups and asked to make up a routine to a piece of music. From time to time, Elaine and Shelly looked up from their close conversation at various girls; they nodded and smiled before talking again.

Halfway through the class, Elaine stood and said, 'See some of you on future castings. Keep up the good work,' and with that she was gone.

***

In subsequent classes, we learnt how to hold and present ourselves in front of clients, and found out how to apply make-up naturally, in a way that let our natural beauty shine through. Shelly drummed this into our heads, because she didn't want to see foundation lines round our faces and neck, or unnecessary, heavy make-up applied round our eyes and lips.

During one of the classes, I needed the toilet. On my way through reception, I bumped into Robert, who was just leaving his office. He spontaneously grabbed hold of my arm, which startled me; he raised it up high enough that I thought he was going to twirl me around. I noticed his firm grip and was aware that I didn't try to pull away, because I froze, wondering what he was going to do next.

His eyes glimmered and he said, 'If you keep an eye on the way you look now, you'll be very successful in the industry.' He pulled himself away, still holding my arm, and explored my body with his eyes before releasing me.

I smirked and wandered to the toilet. Even though I felt a little weird from the way he had looked at me, my self-esteem was boosted by me seeing into my own future. I was certainly on the right road to becoming a professional model.

***

I attended the classes each week, without fail, apart from when classes were closed at Christmas. I'd return home satisfied, and expressing to my parents how much I enjoyed the classes and that I was making new friends. They were happy because they knew where I was and because I wasn't roaming the streets of Manchester aimlessly.

The news that Leanne and I had started modelling classes had gone round the school. I didn't like this fact, and I knew it was Gemma who had spread the news because she had joined the modelling agency soon after Leanne and I did. The boys teased us by saying I was too skinny, Leanne wasn't that pretty and Gemma was going to start modelling spot cream. We ignored their banter, which was thankfully only short lived; this was because both Leanne and Gemma left the agency a few months later. They weren't enjoying the classes as much I was, and so the people in school assumed that, because they had left, I had too.

This was a significant time for me of slowly drifting away from old friends; I felt the need to latch on somewhere else, and the best option was the modelling agency. I started to establish a new peer group away from my community and I gained a deeper sense of belonging. It gave me an exciting outlook towards the glamorous world of modelling and what I could gain from it. I also had older people to help develop a new part of me and to help me to grow up to be like them. (Who needed teenage magazines when I had real models to look up to!)

I began to feel less pressured to perform in school; I didn't excel in academic work. I was creative and sporty, and loved art and athletics, but I realised they weren't going to get me anywhere in life, and certainly wouldn't help me to travel the world and buy a house. The whole modelling-agency experience was intoxicating, with Gina and Robert building up my self-esteem for my future. However, I was unaware that I was falling victim to its predators.

Reflection

During the early phases of the grooming process, the abuser takes an interest in their target and a relationship is formed. This imitates a genuine, positive relationship to make the victim feel special. Robert was cunning in gaining an advantage over his targets; he knew that, in the future, he could coerce his prey into doing anything he wanted.

Robert and Gina were seen as mentors who would play an important part in my future career, which showed my parents how I could benefit from the relationship. This is typical in the grooming process. Perpetrators win over the child and the family's trust, which makes it more difficult for a child to disclose any sexual abuse. This friendliness encourages the child to let their guard down, and it's during this phase that the offender is constantly watching from the shadows, and taking note of the child's vulnerabilities and needs. A small percentage of child molesters are known to target innocent and trusting minors, who they can slowly prepare to be exploited. I was a child needing guidance and attention, and – once Robert established this – he used it to his advantage.

The subtle grooming behaviours are difficult to identify at the beginning because they're made to look like normal adult-child interactions. Please take note and consider anything that seems odd, especially any touching, such as an arm around the shoulder, a tap on the leg or a simple cuddle. In my case, Robert's tight grip of my arm and the way he looked at me overstepped the adult-child boundary. However, him priming me with words obscured his inappropriate behaviour. In any instances of touching where there's a considerable age gap between those involved, I'd be curious about the intentions of the one doing the touching, and question it with a safe adult or friend.

3

FALLING INTO THE TRAP

In the spring of 1991, I felt a little lost after the death of my gran during the winter months. My family home seemed quieter than normal, and I found myself going out at every opportunity. Each week, the modelling agency came as a welcome distraction from this loss.

When I turned 14, I received a certificate from them stating that I had attended a beauty and fashion course, had passed the intermediate-level practical examinations and had been awarded a grade A. Even though Robert quickly presented me with the certificate as I left the office, I noticed it was signed by the head booker who wasn't around. I was pleased with myself and held the certificate with pride as I travelled home alone on the bus. I was determined to keep going no matter how long it took to achieve my goal.

It wasn't long after this that I began to attend the Saturday classes from 11am–5pm, and stay all day Sunday. I knew many people there, and gradually joined the group of popular girls. I had become devoted to it now that I was part of the team. The whispers in the back of my mind kept telling me that I was going to leave school and become a professional model, and Northern Teen Models was my saviour. Shelly was impressed with my dedication, and spoke with Gina and Robert about my working all day Sunday. They agreed, and my job description was to make drinks for them and sign the girls in on their arrival. I was paid £10, which was welcome, as by this time I had begun to smoke much more and needed the extra cash.

Northern Teen Models gave me stability, and I looked forward to Saturday mornings, when I taught the girls basic steps and helped build their confidence. I was grateful to Gina and Robert for allowing me to have this experience, and they soon gave me the added responsibility of answering the phones during the weekend. These calls were normally from parents or the girls, confirming whether or not they were attending the classes. It was around this time that I was trying not to frequently ask my parents for money. I still worked for Leanne's stepfather the odd time; however, I was becoming increasingly dependent on the money I received from the modelling agency each week.

***

One Sunday afternoon, when the classes had finished, I waited patiently for Robert to surface from his office to pay me; 30 minutes had passed since the last person had left.

When he emerged from his room, he looked surprised to see me sitting there. 'Oh, what are you still doing here?' he asked.

I felt embarrassed replying, 'I worked today and I'm waiting to be paid.'

Robert appeared to look puzzled. 'I didn't know you were down for working today,' he said, reaching for the money I had bagged for each class.

I watched as he tipped out the change and counted out my wages; I noticed a few extra quid go in, which I was pleased about. However, I felt uncomfortable standing up and taking the money with his eyes boring into me. I couldn't wait to leave; it felt like he hadn't fully noticed me before this day, and had only seen my outer shell when he stopped me in my tracks to look at my body that time when I ran into him on the way to the toilet.

Now he was looking at me differently, like he was figuring out who I was inside. He opened the door while saying goodbye, and I got in the lift and descended in it, perplexed by the weird energy between us and wondering what was going on in his mind. (I believe this was the time Robert recognised he had something I needed, and noted this dependence on him. I unknowingly fell into the trap that would allow Robert to groom me.)

***

The months flew by, and each week I sat with my new friends, waiting for Shelly to begin the class.

'Hi ladies, before we start, Gina wants to say something to you all,' Shelly said as she turned the music off and waved through the glass door to reception for Gina to enter.

Gina looked radiant as she stood before us. She explained, 'Hi girls, we've booked a photographer to come in and take some professional photos of you. The photoshoot will take place during a week day. There will be a small fee, but you'll receive a mini book and prints to start you off in us promoting you for castings for jobs.' Gina observed us closely.

The room was full of excited energy and sparkling eyes.

'Please go home and ask your parents about this, then call me, and I'll give you a day and time for the shoot.' Gina scanned the room and smiled at our happy faces.

Wow, professional photos, I thought; I had dreamt of this

moment since the first day I had stepped into the modelling agency and looked through the models' portfolios. I was eager to get home and ask my parents. I knew they would have some questions before they agreed for me to take the afternoon off school. They could see how much I loved the classes, and I had spoken many times about having professional photos done. My feet were now firmly in place to walk into the life of a model, and there was no turning back.

***

My dream became a reality when the day of the photoshoot arrived.

I hadn't been to the modelling agency during the week and didn't know what to expect. I wondered if I'd bump into Elaine and see her in action at the booking desk. I was curious about her because one of the older girls – Poppy, who helped out in reception on Saturdays – told me that Robert had described Elaine as being paranoid and feisty. Once Elaine got so angry that she destroyed an intercom monitor in the office and screamed that it was being tapped by Robert. Poppy had looked over my head as I sat facing her at the reception desk, and pointed with her eyes as if to indicate the intercom she destroyed. I looked up to find a small monitor in the corner, and was surprised I hadn't noticed it before when I sat signing in the girls.

When I arrived on the day of the photoshoot, I slipped into the quiet reception, which was so unlike it usually was in the hustle and bustle of the weekend classes. There was no Elaine, which was different to what I imagined, so I followed the music and voices into the catwalk room. I opened the door wider, and found crisp, white sheets draped from the ceiling and over the floor, and lights on stands stood on either side, shining on the backdrop.

The photographer introduced himself, saying, 'Hi, I'm Danny; it's nice to meet you,' and he held out his hand for me to shake.

'Hi, I'm Claire,' I replied in a meek voice, shaking his hand. I was relieved when I saw Gina and Shelly were sitting on the massage table at the back of the room, doing hair and make-up.

'Hi Claire, sit down and I'll do you next. I'm nearly finished here,' Gina shouted over the music.

I sat, content in the knowledge that Gina would do my make-up; my infatuation with her had grown since day one, and I so wanted to be like her in every way.

It wasn't long before Gina yelled, 'Claire, I'm ready for you now; come and sit here.' Gina waved for me to sit in front of her.

I walked over to her grinning face, and sat on the chair between her legs.

Gina began gently massaging moisturiser into my skin. 'Were your parents and teachers OK for you to take the afternoon off school?' Gina asked.

'Yeah, I wasn't doing much in school, anyway. I don't like many lessons,' I confirmed. I felt like a little girl, looking doe-eyed at her.

'You have beautiful skin,' Gina added, as she patted it with a tissue and looked lovingly at me.

'Thank you,' I replied. I wasn't used to being complimented, and my cheeks blushed from this flattery. I could hear the clicking of the camera as I sat quietly, wondering what was happening behind the white backdrop. I wanted to get up and watch, because I hadn't a clue how to pose in front of the camera.

'OK, Claire, I'm finished with your make-up. I'll do a touch up when you're behind the camera,' Gina stated, then leant back and looked admiringly at her work.

I turned to look in the mirror and saw a transformed young lady staring back.

'Jump up and let's get an outfit on you,' suggested Gina. She walked to the open suitcase on the floor and started to pull clothes out.

'You have so many nice clothes,' I responded enviously, looking at the garments that were strewn to the side as Gina looked feverishly for something.

'Here, try this on,' she said, giving me a light-brown lace dress with ivory satin underneath the lace.

I went to the changing room and noticed some boxes and chairs had been removed from around the filing cabinet, making the room much brighter and more spacious. I slipped into the long dress and walked from the room, feeling a little shy.

Gina examined me and stated, 'It fits perfectly, but I'm not happy with the length.' She approached and lifted the bottom of the dress above my knees. 'I think it'll look better short. What do you reckon, Shelly?'

'I agree,' Shelly replied, glancing over the head of the girl whose make-up she was doing.

Gina found a pair of scissors and cut the pretty dress above my knees.

I gasped, 'Are you sure?'

'Well, it's too late now,' Gina exclaimed, as she got up from kneeling on the floor with part of the dress in her hand. 'Sit down and I'll do your hair.'

Gina fiddled for a while before pulling my hair to the side in a neat plait to finish the whole look.

'You look stunning, Claire, and a little bit oriental,' Shelly commented.

These compliments were making me feel good and uncomfortable at the same time. 'Thank you,' I said coyly. It made a change from the tracksuits I wore and the make-up I hadn't quite mastered on myself.

My stomach turned when Danny said, 'I'm ready for you now, Claire'.

I stepped onto the backdrop, stood in front of the camera and froze. Danny could tell I needed some guidance and shouted Gina over. I felt awkward with my rigid movements, and tried to mirror Gina the best I could.

'Just relax and try to be natural with your poses,' Danny said confidently pointing his camera at me.

Yes, it's easy for you to say, I thought.

Danny seemed impatient, and ended up telling me where to stand and look before he asked for another outfit change.

After the shoot, Gina asked if I needed to remove my make-up, but I chose not to because I wanted to show off my transformation at home. When I returned home, I kept looking at myself in the mirror, not wanting to take the beautiful mask off, and envisioned myself on the front covers of magazines.

***

A few weeks later, on my original Sunday class, Robert entered the catwalk room with 6x8-inch, red mini books. These were the first books that were given to models just starting out at Northern Teen Models. Robert asked Shelly to turn the music down and told us to look through the portfolios.

He raised one and said, 'Claire Gray, you should be proud of these pictures. You look great, and you new girls should look up to her – she is going to be successful one day.'

My stomach flipped as he handed the books round before walking over to present me with mine. Robert winked before turning away. I felt very special from that moment on and was ecstatic at having my first professional photos in front of me.

When I opened the first page, Robert stood at the door and said, 'Hand your book round so the others can see,' then left and closed the door behind him.

Although I couldn't wait to get home and show my parents, I wasn't so enthusiastic about showing the girls in the class; however, I was grateful for the praise I received when I did what was asked. (This was the beginning of me complying with what Robert wanted, because I saw him as a key figure to my future dreams coming true.)

I leapt into life and walked in front of the girls. It was good to be part of the team. My confidence grew more in that day than any other I had spent at Northern Teen Models, and I had Gina and Robert to thank for that. Even if there was competition within the environment, we worked well together.

After the class, I rushed to leave the modelling agency and as I stepped into the lift Robert stopped me.

'Bring your book back next week,' he said. 'It needs to stay here so we can begin to show your pictures to clients.'

I nodded in agreement, pressed the button for the lift to descend and watched his smiling face go out of sight.

I practically ran home and bounced into the house, saying, 'Look what I've got!' as I passed my portfolio to my mum.

'These are good pictures, Claire,' she said looking through them.

'I can't wait to show Leanne and the girls in school tomorrow,' I added, taking it from her hands.

'Keep it safe. You don't want to lose it,' my mum warned me as she carried on cooking the Sunday roast.

'I won't lose this book, Mum; maybe a school book, but not this,' I confirmed. I excitedly sat down to take another look at the girl staring back at me.

***

The following day, I walked to school feeling proud and waited for the right moment to show my friends. However, I felt a little apprehensive because I was unsure of people's reactions towards the new path I was taking. During drama class, I finally shared my portfolio. The teachers were impressed, wished me luck and told me to go for it. Leanne was happy for me, even though she said she had no desire to go back to the modelling agency when I asked her.

***

In September 1991, I started Year 10. Now that I had a mini book, copies of my pictures were sent to the photographers' studios in both the city centre and Ardwick Green to begin promoting me for work. My first casting was for a bridal show, and my parents allowed me to take another afternoon off school for it. I didn't have to worry about what I was going to wear, because Gina told me she would bring something in of hers. I appreciated her thoughtful kindness. However, I knew she didn't want me attending a casting in my favourite Puma tracksuit. Gina told me to arrive at the modelling agency early, so I could change and meet some of the professionals models.

When I arrived, the building was bustling with models; I had never seen the office so busy, and I finally got to meet Elaine up close and personal. I changed into a simple summer dress in the back room, and Gina took me to her room to apply some natural make-up. Robert seemed to have a spring in his step because the place was full. He was laughing and joking with some of the older girls as I walked towards the catwalk room, which was now full of models. I watched them let their hair down, apply their make-up and swap from flats to heeled shoes. The competition looked fierce; the girls were gorgeous and full of character. I stayed mute, listening to the banter; I sat there feeling inadequate compared to them and wondered if I could do this as a job when it made me so self-conscious.

Elaine asked to see the new girls walk, and she observed as we strutted up and down the room towards her, one by one. I felt her eyes bore into my body, scrutinising my every move.

'OK, thank you, but please don't do many turns; just concentrate on walking and smile at the clients,' Elaine said firmly.

I breathed a sigh of relief as we walked away and squashed into the back room, waiting for the clients to arrive.

Gina stood at the door, supervising us going out one by one. She started with a few professionals before sending the novices out next. When I heard my name, I just wanted to jump out of the open window into the smelly back alley below.

'Claire, get ready; the other girl is nearly finished,' Gina said hurriedly.

I squeezed through the overcrowded room and waited beside Gina. I felt much worse about going out for the second time, with Elaine's words ringing in my ears and knowing I had to face the clients' scrutiny. I emerged from the room with a smile and felt a nervous twitch from my mouth, which I was sure they could see as I walked towards the three clients and Elaine, who were all sitting behind the long, grey table that had been brought in from reception. I walked up and down, then Elaine cued me to finish by raising her eyebrows. My hopes about being chosen for the job were lifted when the clients narrowed their selection and asked some of us to do a routine to see who worked well together. Elaine told us to do the walk for eight, which gave me some confidence because I could do this catwalk routine in my sleep.

After the casting, I made my way through the streets of Longsight; it was beginning to feel as though I was living in two worlds. At the modelling agency, I was living the dream of many girls and I felt lucky to be on the right road to making something of my life. But it was as if I were a new girl walking round my neighbourhood, looking and feeling different from how I was before. I was heading in a completely different direction from the people I knew, and this feeling of being in between my old self and my potential future self was unsettling.

I waited anxiously by the phone for the next few days, praying that Gina would say they had chosen me. Unfortunately, I was to be disappointed when she told me they liked me, but thought I was too young and skinny for what they were looking for.

***

One evening when the dark nights were drawing in, I received an urgent phone call from Gina asking if I could make it into town and attend a casting for a top hairdresser. Tony had won a few hairdressing awards in the North of England, and he needed someone for a hair show from 6.30pm for a couple of hours.

Gina said, 'It'll only be you and another model, Robin, going to see him. He'll tell you there and then if he wants you.'

I felt a little anxious, and I told Gina I'd have to ask my parents.

'If he likes you, you'll be working until 8.30pm,' she confirmed.

I left the phone off the receiver while I asked my parents for permission.

'A hair show. It's a bit late to be asking now!' Dad exclaimed.

'I might get the job because there are only two of us going,' I added.

'OK, but your brother will have to go with you. You're not going to town alone when its dark outside,' Dad replied. He shouted to my older brother to come down from upstairs, and – when my brother came down – Dad told him he had to accompany me into the city centre and wait with me if I got the job.

I confirmed to Gina that I had permission, and my brother and I set off.

Even though I was with my brother, I felt a little frightened as we made our way to the Manchester Piccadilly Hotel, because it was dark and there was a different vibe in town. When we reached the hotel reception, I nervously asked for Tony. He emerged from a conference room and introduced himself. I felt intimidated as he rummaged through my hair; I could tell it wasn't in good condition because of the perm I had and it was starting to fall out. Tony kindly told me I wasn't right for what he was looking for, and that the other girl had arrived first, and her hair was thicker for him to cut and play around with. I had never felt so small and rejected, even though he thanked me for coming at such short notice.

My brother tried to cheer me up on the bus ride home, but to no avail. I started to doubt myself and again wondered if this was what I wanted to do, knowing that nine times out of ten I'd be turned down for work. Gina later reassured me that it wasn't me, that these rejections were part of the job and everything I did was helping me gain more experience, even though it didn't seem like it at the time.

***

I went into school the following day with a dark cloud hanging over my head; I felt alone in my own little world. It was the only morning I didn't have my wits about me, and I walked into a situation I had no control over and where I had no one for back up when older bullies targeted me. I was walking along the outdoor corridor to reach my form room, and – as I approached the main building and stretched out my hand to open the door – a group of girls stepped in front of me. My heart sank when I faced a large girl who was staring at me menacingly; some boys were standing in the background, and I became aware that I was in some sort of danger and my career flashed before me.

Even though I was shitting myself, I stood my ground. I was relieved and felt a little safer when I recognised a girl who hung out with my elder brother.

However, the large girl shouted to another, 'Get her now!'

I was puzzled by the lack of reaction and words from the others, and looked towards my brother's friend for an answer. The bully stepped closer still, guarding the entrance. But still no one did anything.

'Well, go on then, do something,' the large girl screeched, seemingly annoyed that no one was reacting.

I had no clue what was going on; I could fight if I needed to, but not five against one.

Finally, the tension was diffused when one of the boys shouted over, 'Leave it out, Kaz.' (Kaz being the large girl in question.)

Kaz turned to face me again, saying, 'Right, then, I'll sort this. You dare go out with Jamie, and I'll knock you out. He is my mate's man, OK!' The venom in her voice made her spit in the air between us.

I opened the door without speaking but breathed a sigh of relief and walked quickly to my classroom, thinking about Jamie pursuing me. I always knocked him back, and even if I were free and interested in the future, I'd carry on saying no because I didn't want Kaz on top of me, pulling my hair out.

It was moments like this when I couldn't wait to leave school. I was relieved I had the modelling agency as a fallback, and knowing this made difficult situations at school easier to bear, due to my life being mapped out in the modelling world. I thought that maybe some people hated me for this new pathway I was on, and – as a result of this incident – I began to read others closely and became acutely aware of the girls I needed to steer clear of. I couldn't afford to be beaten, because my face and body were now the tools of my trade.

Reflection

A round this time in the grooming process, the abuser builds on the positive relationship already established in the earlier phase. At age 14, I had no idea that I was falling into the trap of a paedophile's world. These teenage years are a highly stimulating phase, and a time where teens need plenty of guidance and understanding. A groomer's aim is to keep building trust; this is the central role of the grooming process, so they can become key figures in their victim's life. My abusers gained power over me by promising me a bright future, which meant my guard was down, and I became dependent on them for money, and for the building of my confidence and responsibilities around the modelling agency. Experiencing this was a distraction from what was really happening behind the scenes in his private office.

Grooming is a gradual, methodical process and can go on for years without any inappropriate behaviour occurring. Time wasn't an issue to my offender (nor to many others) because, no matter how long it took, he would eventually reach his goal of gratifying his need for young girls. Robert was skilled at selecting those most desirable to prepare for abuse, because he had done it many times before.

During this phase, like Robert, most offenders show a warm and caring side, and acts of kindness, both verbally or materially. These are all behaviours calculated to lead their victims closer to becoming more compliant, and more of a willing participant in the exchanges between the abuser and the abused. This is key to keeping the grooming process active for when the sexual abuse starts to occur. If you're experiencing something similar to this phase, this would be the point to remove yourself, so the offender can't manipulate you further.

4

BLURRED BOUNDARIES

At the beginning of 1992, life became more exciting. My weekends were full of modelling-agency commitments, and the evenings were taken up with hanging out with friends. I had an admirer where I lived and I liked the fact he didn't attend my school. Sean's handsome looks had many girls chasing him, and wherever I hung out he popped up when I least expected it. To my delight, Sean showed up at the swimming baths one evening, wanting to accompany me home. My friends giggled, said goodbye and left me at the bus stop with him. I was nervous because he had asked me persistently for months to be his girlfriend and now he had me cornered.

'You know I really like you, Claire, and have for a long time; may I just kiss you now?'

I was lost for words for a moment as we gazed into each other's eyes. He wasn't going to take no for an answer.

'Here and now?' I finally replied.

'Well, we can go behind the swimming baths,' he added, smiling cheekily.

I thought I needed to do this; I had kept him waiting long enough. 'Oh, all right then, dick,' I blurted out. *All right, dick*, I repeated in my head. I was mortified that this had slipped from my mouth and began to feel my cheeks burn from my nervous outburst.

'OK,' Sean replied, puzzled and seemingly hurt by my stupid name calling.

I stood up from the bench, embarrassed. 'Shall we go now? I don't want to miss the bus home. My parents will be expecting me for tea,' I added quickly, wanting to forget what I'd just said.

Walking towards the swimming baths, I looked at Sean coyly; there was no doubt we had a spark between us. Reaching the back of Gorton Tub, we found ourselves alone, and Sean took my hand and gently but firmly walked me up against the wall. His confidence felt exciting, and he kissed me so passionately that I felt weak at the knees.

I pulled away, 'Sorry for—'

Sean didn't let me finish my sentence and pushed his lips onto mine again.

God, he is so good at this, I thought, *Could he be the one? He is a dream and we are a perfect fit.* I drew back. 'I need to go home; my mum will ground me if I'm late,' I said, gazing into his sparkling, dark eyes.

'Just one more, Claire,' he said and pulled me back to him.

'Stop, let's go now,' I stated, putting up a feeble fight.

We decided to walk home, and by this point I didn't care if I got into trouble for returning home late. We walked the streets dreamily, hand in hand, and I felt safe walking along the path that made me fearful at times.

When we reached my front door, Sean asked, 'Will you be my girlfriend now?'

I smiled. How could I refuse his handsome face? 'Yes,' I replied kissing him on the cheek.

Sean pulled me close and said, 'See you tomorrow, my beautiful girl'.

Sean and I were inseparable for months. I was very happy having a future I could see into clearly. I had a boyfriend I was crazy about, and the modelling classes would turn me into a model who would travel the world one day – life couldn't get any better.

***

Early one Saturday morning, Sean and I hung out before I started the usual classes.

'Do you have to go to the modelling agency today?' Sean asked, wanting me to stay with him for the day.

'Yes, I do; I get paid for working there,' I confirmed. I opened Sean's garden gate to leave and he gently pulled at my arm.

'You can miss it for one day,' he pleaded. Sean cupped my cheeks with his hands and tried to kiss me into staying.

'Stop it. We can meet later this evening, like we planned; I'll come straight to you after the classes,' I replied. Then I walked onto the pavement and blew him a kiss goodbye. I hadn't missed many classes, and the only time I couldn't attend was when I had family holidays.

I made my way to the modelling agency, and a little while after I'd arrived I sat chatting with Cassandra about Sean. She asked what he looked like, and I described him lovingly, 'He has the most amazing skin and dark-brown eyes, we've known of each other for years and have been exclusive for months… We've spoken about going all the way.'

I waited for any reaction from Cassandra before carrying on; she remained observant.

'I want to wait until I'm 16 though, but he wants to do it now...' my voice trailed off into thought and it crossed my mind whether I should ask Cassandra if she had experienced sex; after all, she was 16.

'So you haven't done anything with anyone yet?' Cassandra asked curiously, breaking the silence.

'No way; I've only kissed boys. I know I'm nearly 15, but 14 is too young,' I said indignantly. 'Have you?' I fired back.

'Yes, I have,' Cassandra's eyes twinkled, and mine widened.

'Who with? What was it like? Is it painful? Did you bleed?' I wanted to gather as much information as possible.

Cassandra answered with a chuckle, 'I used to hang out with a large group of friends a few years back, and I slept with one of the boys a few times. It was nothing serious, and now I'm here.' Cassandra wasn't able to say any more because Robert opened his office door, making me jump.

'Will you make me a coffee, Claire? Just the way I like it,' Robert asked, then he lit the cigarette hanging from his mouth and passed it to Cassandra. I found it unpleasant when he chewed the end of his cigarette and passed it to those of us who smoked; we would take it without protesting at his saliva being drooled over the stub.

'Would you like a cigarette, Claire?' he asked, and pulled one from the pack knowing I'd take it.

'Yes, please,' I said.

Robert placed one beside the ashtray as I left reception. I stood waiting for the kettle to boil, caught a glimpse through the window of Cassandra and Robert talking intimately, and wondered what they were saying. It was clear to see their relationship was one of mutual fondness. Their conversation stopped as I entered reception and passed Robert his coffee.

'Thank you, Claire; smoke your cigarette and then rejoin the class. Cassandra may stay out here.' He headed back to his office and closed the door.

I sat down and lit my cigarette; I felt grown up doing this, even though my parents would be disappointed to find out that I smoked.

'So, do you think you'll sleep with Sean?' Cassandra quickly asked in a prying way, like she needed to gather as much information as she could before I left.

'Well, this evening we're meeting up. His aunt's house is empty for the weekend, and we're gonna hang out with a group of friends,' I explained. I felt a little embarrassed when Cassandra raised her eyebrow in a knowing way, which made me uncomfortable. I took another drag of my cigarette and blew out the smoke, which filled the air between us, before stubbing the cigarette out. 'I can say no, you know,' I stated, and I stood to rejoin the class, which ended the conversation.

***

Later that day, I left the modelling agency, wondering how the evening would progress. Although I was in some denial of what lay ahead, the night had been planned for some time. I kept saying to myself that I could say no if I didn't want to go along with something, especially sex.

When I got to Sean's aunt's house, I knocked on the door and waited anxiously for him to answer; I wanted to get the evening over with.

'Hey babe.' Sean beamed as he let me in.

'Hi,' I replied. I walked behind him and wondered if this boy I adored would take my virginity.

'How were the classes today?' he said.

I loved the fact he asked questions and showed an interest in what I did. 'They were good; I had a new girl to teach. Where is everyone?' I queried as I took my coat off and sat down.

'They're coming later with some drinks,' he confirmed. Sean sat next to me and looked into my eyes.

I thought he was so good to look at, as he was so handsome. We kissed, and he was soon lying on top of me.

'Stop it, Sean; the others will be here soon,' I said and playfully pushed him away.

Sean stood and pulled a packet of condoms from his pocket. I stared and thought how responsible he was. Even though I knew what to expect, I started to get nervous; I didn't know how I'd respond to the act of actually going through with sex.

'It'll be OK,' Sean added trying to reassure me. He seemed to sense what was on my mind, and gently pulled me in for a kiss and stroked my hair.

My thoughts were running wild. How would I feel and see myself after losing my virginity? What if it got round the school? I could be called a slag. And what would my parents think if they realised what I was about to do? Sex was such a taboo subject with them. I shook my head to try to release the tension. Anyway, my parents didn't have to know. I just wished that I understood a little more about it, because I didn't want to disappoint Sean.

Sean led me upstairs, and as we entered the bedroom he gently asked, 'Shall we keep the lights on or off?'

'Off,' I quickly replied. There was no way I needed to see myself embarrassed from my inexperience of what we were about to do.

Sean closed the curtains, and all we could see were the outlines of our bodies from the light shining through the curtains. I froze for a moment, contemplating the next move. Sean strode over and hugged me before planting kisses round my face. It felt right, and I started to get lost in the moment and fell to the bed with him. We kissed and caressed under the covers; I wanted this to carry on, but his hard crotch began to distract me as it pushed against my thigh. I responded by pushing my hips upwards. I was hot, but I didn't know whether it was from nerves or excitement from our passion for one another.

Sean stood and removed his pants. I followed by slipping mine off under the bed covers and dropped them to the floor. He reached for the condoms, ripped one open and slipped it onto his erection. I sat up with my eyes fixed on his penis. This was the first erection I had seen; I couldn't stop looking at it and wondered how the hell it'd fit into me. I felt tense and wondered if I could go through with it.

Sean gently guided me back onto the bed and lay on top of me. 'Are you ready?' he said searching for my eyes in the dim light.

'I think so,' I replied, staring at his silhouette and thinking, *Why can't we just carry on kissing?* My mind wanted to go through with it, but my body was tightening underneath him as he swirled against me, trying to find a rhythm. Sean pushed his erection between my legs, searching for a way to get inside me. We tried for a while, but I was too tense to take it to the next level.

'Help me here; it's not happening,' Sean exclaimed, frustrated. He rose and looked down at me.

'I'm sorry, I can't do it,' I whispered. I couldn't see Sean's face clearly, but I knew he was disappointed.

We lay kissing for a while, and I was relieved when I heard a knock at the front door. We quickly dressed and headed downstairs to hang out with our friends. I was a bit confused about how I felt about my virginity remaining unbroken, and I wondered how Sean felt about me now, because he became distant during the evening. (This was a moment in time that I'd look back on wistfully, wishing he was the one who took my virginity. I felt safe and not pressured by Sean to carry on with something I wasn't ready to do, unlike later, when my guard was down, I was under the influence of alcohol and let an abuser force themselves onto me.)

***

The following day, I was almost late arriving at the modelling agency, as I had overslept and had to dash from the house. I hated to be late for things and was surprised I still got there on time. I quickly changed into my bathing suit, while replaying the night before over in my head. I hoped Sean was OK; I knew his friends would tease him if they found out we tried to take each other's virginity and it didn't work out the way we imagined.

In between classes, Robert began fishing for information about my family background, but more about what I did socially. (I believe he was probing into my private life for the satisfaction of knowing I was still a virgin.) At the time, it didn't seem like probing; it was more like he was taking a genuine interest in my life, although I wondered what his agenda was when he began to judge the areas I hung out in. Robert turned his nose up at them and told me they were rough areas, and he added that people should mix with their own kind. I listened, and kept quiet about me dating Sean, who was mixed race. However, my mind drifted to Cassandra, and I wondered whether she had told Robert about Sean; he didn't need to know what I was up to in my private time with friends, surely? Robert swiftly changed the conversation to my future career, which always pleased me, and I forgot all about his probing and comments about my community. (I later came to believe that this conversation prompted my invitation into their private world.)

***

One day at the end of spring, I was sitting in reception when a smiling Gina left Robert's office. It crossed my mind that I'd only stepped into his room a handful of times, to give him coffee or a phone message. Other than that, his door was always closed and locked when he wasn't around.

Gina beamed and said, 'Claire, we were wondering if you'd like to stay at the models' house on Saturdays with me, Robert and some of the other girls?'

I grinned from cheek to cheek; Gina could clearly see it was a yes.

'When the last class has finished on Saturday, we go for dinner – our favourite restaurant is our local Chinese – and sometimes we'll go to the cinema or theatre before heading back to the house. On Sundays, we attend an aerobics class,' Gina explained.

She didn't have to try to sell me anything; I was already sold on the idea.

'I'd love to,' I said excitedly; I now felt like one of the special girls.

'When you get home, ask your parents for permission and call me. I think you'll enjoy staying with us; you'll come along so well – not that you haven't already,' Gina said.

She then stood and joined the class, while I sat contentedly in reception, contemplating my fate.

***

At the end of the day, I dashed home and told Mum about the models' house.

'Where is it?' she asked curiously.

'It's in Altrincham somewhere,' I told her. I didn't care much for details; I was just happy that Gina had asked me to stay with the regular girls. 'We'll go for dinner and sometimes to the cinema, but we'll mainly hang out and pamper ourselves at the house; it's all part of the training,' I explained. I willed her to say yes.

'OK, I'll call Gina and have a chat,' she replied.

'Please say yes, Mum. I'm in safe hands, as Robert is an ex-police officer,' I pleaded. I stared into Mum's eyes as I persisted in trying to get my own way. I was sure that she would agree after this last statement I'd made. Robert had told us he had served as a police officer and was a man to be trusted.

'We'll see, Claire. I need to speak with your father and then call Gina,' stated Mum.

The conversation ended, but I knew they couldn't refuse what I wanted to do.

***

The following weekend, I didn't have to rush home because my parents had agreed to let me stay at the models' house. Gina had told them I'd be staying there with other girls, and that this was all part of the training to get girls used to being away from home when they became models and started to work abroad.

I happily waited with the others in reception, observing the lively banter, as I watched the last class of girls leave.

Robert emerged from his office in a jolly manner, saying, 'Claire and Beth, we need to call your parents.'

Beth and I looked at each other puzzled.

'Don't worry; I need to ask if you may have a glass of wine with your meal tonight; I don't want to get on the wrong side of your parents. You make the call for Gina,' Robert said and smiled crookedly.

I dialled my parents number and passed Gina the phone. As she spoke to them, she sounded so alluring, and I knew my parents had agreed.

'Well, that's all okayed,' Gina said, replacing the receiver and looking in Robert's direction.

After the same phone call was repeated to Beth's parents, we left the office in laughter, and I felt like a confirmed member of the group. I was happy to be with people who fully accepted me; after all, we were in the same boat. Robert chose which girls travelled in each car to the restaurant; I secretly wished to go with Gina.

'Claire, Beth, Karen and Cassandra you're with Gina, the rest of you come with me,' he commanded.

We obediently did as we were told. I loved the flash sports cars they drove; I'd never been in one before. This whole experience of becoming acquainted with the high life was very enticing.

***

A short time later, we entered the Chinese restaurant they raved about, and I was struck by the amount of people looking up from their meals to watch seven attractive girls follow Robert and Gina to the back of the restaurant. It was like he owned the place; he nodded to the manager and sat at the round table.

Again, people glanced curiously over at us.

'Hello Robert, how are you? Is it the usual to start with?' the manager asked, looking round the table.

'I'm well, thanks, Ken. Yes, the usual, please, and an extra bottle to be chilled, as we have two new girls staying with us. These are Claire and Beth,' confirmed Robert.

I smiled, picked up the menu to scan it and wondered what I could order.

However, there wasn't any choice because Robert dominated the scene and said, 'I'll order a bit of everything. It's easier this way because we can share the different dishes, unless there's something you can't eat, in which case I'll order a dish that you do like.'

I wasn't about to lay down any demands at this point, so I put the menu down and surveyed the faces before me. We were all pretty girls, and most of us were the same age, apart from Karen, who was a year younger, and Cassandra, who was almost two years older.

Ken returned with bottles of Asti Martini and Robert's Diet Coke, and asked, 'Shall I pour, Robert?'

'No, I'll do it, Ken; also, will you make the usual to start with?' Robert said, taking the bottle from Ken.

'Yes, certainly, sir,' Ken replied and left the table.

I watched Robert pour everyone a drink, apart from himself, and thought, *What a good role model for not drinking.*

'OK, girls, cheers, and welcome to the team, Claire and Beth!' Robert grinned creepily, taking in each one of us with his eyes.

'Cheers,' we added clinking our glasses together. I sipped at the bubbles and thought it made a nice change from the nights in the park drinking White Lightning and strawberry Mad

Dog 20/20. I started to feel more like a lady on a path towards stardom, because I had two adults to guide me and they held the key to unlock my future.

***

En route to the house after the meal, I looked out the car window and thought how far it seemed; there weren't many buildings I recognised as we headed further out of town. We arrived eventually, and Gina parked the car outside a three-storey, semi-detached house. We got out of the car, and – taking my things from the boot – I followed the laughter along the garden path and into the hallway. I mirrored the girls by leaving my bags by the stairs. Gina went straight to the kitchen to put the shopping away. I glanced round the spacious living room that merged into the dining area, and stretched my head to look out the patio doors leading onto the garden. I was unaware that Robert had been watching me.

He smiled saying, 'Gina, show Claire and Beth the house and where they'll be sleeping.' Robert then retired to the living room and switched the TV on.

Beth and I followed Gina to the kitchen, which felt homely and contained a dog that was wagging its tail, wanting a stroke.

'This is Sandy,' Gina said, opening the back door.

The garden stretched back as far as I could see.

'Usually, we have barbecues in the summer,' she said as she closed the door. 'Come this way, and I'll show you the cellar, which we've recently decorated, and made into a mini flat with a living room and bedroom.'

Gina walked ahead of us once more as we followed her into the cellar. She explained, 'If too many girls are staying, some of you may stay down here if you like.'

Gina then headed upstairs with us in tow. 'This is the first bedroom and the en suite bathroom is here,' she said brightly.

I squeezed between the single and double bed, and looked out the balcony door to find Sandy running round the garden.

'Come on, I'll show you the main bathroom,' Gina said, walking from the room.

We followed her to the bathroom, which was dark, and I wondered why the window had been bricked up and painted brown to match the rest of the interior. The steps leading into the bathtub dominated the room. I glanced up and was curious about the light coming from air vents on the wall.

Gina distracted my thoughts by opening a door on the left. 'This is mine and Roberts room,' she explained, leading us in.

Their room had a single bed against the wall with a large double bed pushed against it. I wondered about the single bed and who might sleep in it.

'And this is the dressing room,' Gina said opening another door in the far corner.

I tripped over the weighing scales as I walked through and giggled with Beth.

'We'll weigh you most mornings; Robert is strict about weight,' Gina added.

We followed Gina as she came back out to the main landing and up another flight of stairs; some steps creaked as we made our way up.

'This is the final bedroom,' Gina said proudly. This was my favourite room, and had moonlight shining through the window.

'You two can sleep here with Karen tonight,' she added.

I smiled as Gina led us back downstairs. Being shown round

the house, it seemed like they were trying to sell me something that I didn't have at home.

***

Later that evening, Robert staggered our getting ready for bed; he seemed to like us going up in pairs.

'Claire and Beth, you go up now; you may use the spare bathrobes to lounge in. Also don't be alarmed or feel uncomfortable when you find me with just my underpants on, this is the way I relax,' he said confidently, looking up from the couch.

We stood, and I noticed a glint in his eye that I was unsure how to read as we left the room.

Beth and I returned to find Gina and Cassandra giving Robert a foot and leg massage. I grimaced at his body; his persona reminded me of Henry VIII.

We sat watching TV for a while, and waited patiently for Robert's next move. (It felt like we were pawns in game of chess while we were staying at the house; we couldn't move until we were told and had to ask before we could do things.) I was relieved when he told Beth, Karen and I to go to bed. We chatted and giggled until the early hours before drifting off to sleep.

I liked Karen; she had been with the agency for a year before I started and was the first girl I struck up a conversation with from the group.

***

This first weekend was the start of me becoming a regular at the house. It was a refreshing change from Saturday nights at home, where I was either out or complaining that I didn't have much privacy due to my annoying brothers invading my space. As was typical of many teenage girls, I kept a diary, but this soon came to an end when my brother read them – only to tease me later about the contents – which stopped me from journaling my musings on matters of the heart and everyday life. I felt like I had some privacy when I was at the models' house; however, this didn't make me start writing again. (On reflection, maybe if I'd started I'd have been able to question the odd things that happened, by seeing patterns of behaviour written down.)

We had many fun nights at the house; it was like a pyjama party every weekend. My life had more meaning and purpose, and I felt like I was in safe hands. Sometimes Gina would let us raid her large wardrobe and wear her clothes to the modelling agency. I began transforming from the shell-suit girl into someone who looked mature when I saw my reflection in the mirror. Gina and Robert treated me like an adult, which made me feel older than I was; however, inside I was an impressionable young girl searching for affirmations, which I received from them.

One evening, after getting ready for bed, Robert asked me to go over to him. He gently pulled at my bathrobe before holding my hand and commenting on the cocoa butter I used on my skin.

'Did you know that, in some cultures around the world, some women use cocoa cream to attract men? The smell draws them in,' he said and smiled with his eyes.

With this comment, I felt somewhat in control because I knew I'd never look at him the way he was looking at me.

***

A few weekends later, Karen and I were the only girls staying at the models' house. We were given money and the door keys, and told to get the tram back because Robert had made plans to take a couple of professional models out. They were from the previous group that had stayed at the house and were now in their late teens and early 20s. Robert told us they were driving out of town and would be back late.

When we arrived, we made ourselves at home and were loving the fact we had it to ourselves. Karen experimented on my face using her new make-up, and we washed our hair to try new hairstyles. Karen and I enjoyed each other's company; we were on the same wavelength when having a giggle. We sat up like children waiting for our parents to arrive home, so we could hear all about the evening.

Robert and Gina returned late, with two drunk models in tow. The models stumbled into the kitchen, laughing and asking, 'Hey, girls, what are you two still doing up?'

Dawn was a stunning, 6-foot-tall model whom I had admired from the first day of looking at her portfolio.

'Have you had a nice evening? Poppy and I have, haven't we?' Dawn stated turning to Poppy.

Poppy stayed quiet; I noticed she looked tired and subdued, unlike her usual chatty self.

'Look at you, Claire! Your make-up looks pretty,' Dawn added.

'It's Karen's make-up skills,' I replied, feeling a little intimidated.

Robert entered the kitchen with Gina, and Dawn giggled and said, 'Are you going to take me home now? I need my bed. Or should I jump into one of the beds here?' She went to the fridge and grabbed a bottle of water.

'Dawn, you need to sober up; I can't have any of you being sick in my car.'

Dawn seemed to simmer down and I got the impression he wasn't expecting Karen and I to still be up.

'Gina, sort out the vitamins for Karen and Claire. You girls should head to bed; you must be tired and its late,' he added.

The mood changed and everyone did as they were told. There wasn't much late night talking between Karen and I, and it didn't take long for us to drift off into a deep sleep, leaving the adults chatting downstairs.

Reflection

Reflecting on this chapter, this covered the stage when the building of the relationship increases dramatically, yet remains imbalanced because of the large age gap. Sex offenders aim to stay in a position of having an inappropriate amount of power over their victims, which is used to influence how they behave. The abuser delves for information on the victim's family background and social life, then they insert themselves into their target's life and begin to blur the boundaries.

My groomers began to separate me physically and emotionally from the people closest to me. These people close to the victim are helpful and influential, but pose a threat to the offender. Abusers are usually successful in isolating their victims. My abuser groomed girls in groups, making us feel we were safer with each other, and the girls' parents were led to believe this too. The more an offender cuts off the support network around the victim, the more power they have over the victim because they'll have no one from the outside interfering with their hidden intentions. My abuser was very clever in using his previous job as a police officer to influence how people perceived him; he needed to be seen as a good member of society to impose a false sense of security. This led us girls to think it was OK for a man in his 50s to wear just his underpants and lie on a couch in front of underaged girls.

However, this is all part of a groomer's plan to desensitise the targets so that they feel comfortable with the abuser's semi-nakedness; this leads onto touch, which becomes part of sexualising the relationship in the future. Molesters keep pushing the boundaries when they feel secure that the victim is close enough. My offender gathered information and blurred the boundaries further by holding my hand and telling me how some women attract men. These situations are inappropriate behaviour, and the use of covert sexual comments would ring alarm bells to an outsider looking in.

5

A SEDUCTIVE WORLD

My old friends were becoming part of a distant past, and I drifted away from Sean. Even though we saw each other from time to time, he began to lose interest the more time I spent apart from him. This pained me because I thought he was going to be the one and wait for me. All I could do now was look forward towards my career.

My mini book had progressed to a 9x12-inch portfolio when I had attended a casting for a modelling contract in Japan. I took another afternoon off school to meet a Japanese lady called Yuki, who was a representative for the agencies in Japan. Most of the favourite girls who stayed at the house were at the modelling agency, and I didn't feel threatened like I had on previous castings; these were my friends. We hung out in the catwalk room waiting to see Yuki.

Gina opened the door, making us jump from our conversation. 'Right Claire, you may go first,' she instructed.

'Good luck,' Karen shouted over.

I turned, gritted my teeth into a smile and followed Gina into reception.

'Hi, *konnichiwa*,' Yuki said with a grin.

'Hi,' I said, assuming the Japanese word meant hello or how

are you (I later found it does mean hello). I sat next to Gina, facing Yuki, and watched her look through my portfolio.

Yuki smiled and said in her Japanese accent, 'May I see you in your bathing suit, please?'

'Yes, OK,' I replied and sprang up, wanting to make a good impression with my efficiency; went and quickly got changed; and emerged moments later from the catwalk room.

Yuki stood there with a measuring tape in her hand. 'OK, may I measure you?' she asked.

I nodded, not having much choice. I shot puzzled looks at Gina as Yuki measured the usual requirements of bust, waist and hips, yet went further in measuring my arms, shoulders, legs, hands, wrists and my head. She checked if I had any piercings and asked if I had any tattoos. All this was swiftly done with precision, and the information organised into a file holding composite cards and forms. I had to keep myself from giggling nervously, because I'd never experienced being so thoroughly measured.

'May I take some pictures and a video? I need to show them to the agencies in Japan,' Yuki asked, stretching to her bag and pulling out her cameras.

'Yes, of course you can,' Gina replied before I could agree.

I stood and waited for Yuki to finish filming my portfolio, before she turned, and asked me to stand, introduce myself to the camera and turn round slowly. I did as instructed.

'Thank you, Claire,' said Yuki with a bow.

I grinned at the way she pronounced my name. I mirrored her bow before returning to the others, knowing there was no doubt she liked me.

'How was it, Claire? You were in there a long time,' Karen asked eagerly.

I rolled my eyes to the ceiling jokingly and said, 'Prepare yourself to be measured from head to toe! She takes so many pictures close up, far away, front, back and side, then she videos you doing the same.'

I sat, having a good feeling about the meeting. Although, after the casting, I tried not to attach myself to the outcome, which was to avoid any disappointment if I wasn't offered a contract. So far, people's interest in me had been zero, and this didn't bode well for my future career, nor did it help my self-esteem.

***

However, this soon changed when something happened the following week that caused my confidence to rise to its highest. Yuki had called the modelling agency and told Gina which agencies in Japan had shown an interest in her girls. Gina then called me. I was stunned for a moment as I came off the phone with Gina, as three agencies were interested in me and wanted me to go over as soon as possible. I became ecstatic, thinking how lucky I was and what an opportunity it was, at my age, to travel across the world to Japan. I had dreamt of travelling the world after the first time I went abroad with my parents, and now I had the opportunity to do it by myself.

'Dad, guess what?' I shrieked, as I walked over to stand in front of him, ready to gush about my news, as he sat on the couch.

'Yes, Claire?' he replied staring up at me.

'I'm going to Japan! You know that casting I went to last week? They liked me – well, the agencies in Tokyo did – and they want me to go over as soon as possible. They mentioned me going in the summer holidays for six weeks.'

Dad looked surprised as I carried on, 'They'll prepay everything, such as my accommodation, flights and money to live on each week.' I took a breath, and Dad butted in.

'You're only 15; you have to finish school first,' he said seeming to be in disbelief.

'But, Dad, in the summer I'm not at school,' I protested, even though he had a point.

'You have GCSEs [General Certificates of School Education] to think about and you need to concentrate on your final year. Also, you can't travel all that way by yourself, and we're going to Spain for two weeks in August,' Dad replied.

'But, Dad, I don't like school; I only like athletics and art, and that isn't going to get me anywhere in life. Maybe I could go to Japan for four weeks in August?' I said, still protesting, but knowing I'd have to see out my school education before I travelled the world alone.

'It's best you finish school first, and then if they still want you to go over and you're still interested in going, you may go. But I want to speak with the modelling agency and your mum first,' Dad added.

'OK, but I'll go when I leave school next year,' I said in determined defiance. I'd be patient, even if it killed me, because now I had an aim and the security of guaranteed work when I left school.

***

Towards the end of Year 10, the time came to do work experience. I applied to go to the gas company for two weeks because I wasn't sure what else to do. I told Gina and Robert about my placement, and how disinterested I was in working there. They sat and listened, and their interest in my life made me feel they were acknowledging me.

Robert perked up and queried, 'Why don't you do it here at the modelling agency?'

I looked at him wide-eyed and said, 'Really? But I don't think I can, because it was booked with British Gas a month ago.'

'Yes, but when does it start?' Robert probed.

'In few weeks,' I said, curious about his intent.

'Well, ask your teacher anyway, and see what they say about you doing it here. We'd be more than happy to tell them what we'd require you to do for two weeks,' he confirmed. Robert had that glint in his eye again.

However, I smiled, imagining myself behind the scenes at the agency, learning how it was run during the week. I mused that maybe I could become a booker when my modelling career came to an end.

***

The following week, I headed to the office of Mr Field, the head of year. He happily agreed to change my placement, as he knew I was mapping out a career in modelling. During this time at school, I was more or less on my own, as Leanne had left the school and moved away. I missed our friendship, and had no one to share the modelling world with who would understand like she did. I noticed that most of my friends in school became boys; I hung out with them in the smokers' corner, hoping not to get caught by the teachers before the next lesson started. I could hardly confide in them, and decided to keep modelling-agency business to myself and focus on the new friendships I had gained there.

It was exciting to be entering the adult world for two weeks' work experience, and especially to be doing it at a place I was growing to love, along with the people in it. The more time I spent at the modelling agency, the more I felt grown up and ready to face the adult world.

***

It was a hot summer's morning when I arrived at the office for my first day of work experience. I sat in reception alone until Cassandra walked in from the toilet; she had opened up, and was manning reception until Gina and Robert arrived. I glanced around and wondered what work I'd be doing, because everywhere was tidy and lifeless. The only thing that brought it to life was Robert entering the office in his usual jolly manner.

'Fetch me a coffee, please, Cassandra. I need to make some phone calls. Gina will be up shortly; she is parking the car. Hi Claire,' he said and his eyes sparkled.

Cassandra jumped to his attention.

'Hi Robert,' I said, watching him unlock his door and close it behind him. I mused how he always seemed much busier than the rest of the office.

Robert emerged again with that funny wiggle of his, which made me wonder what was going on his mind.

'Right, girls. Claire, you and Cassandra may go back to the models' house and sunbathe. The office will be quiet today, and Gina and I will stay here.'

I was perplexed; I thought my first day would be spent shadowing Gina in her office. (It never crossed my mind whether this was normal for a Monday morning at the office, with Robert being so sure in his prediction of it being quiet.

After all, I had nothing else to compare it to and was quite happy to chill in the sun for the day.)

Robert suggested I stay at the house for a couple of nights, which pleased me. I told him I needed to go home for a few things and, of course, to ask my parents if I could stay. Robert decided to give me a lift to mine while I ran in for an overnight bag.

'Hi Mum, is it OK for me stay a few nights at the models' house?' I said brightly.

'Claire, I wasn't expecting you home! Shouldn't you be working?' Mum replied.

'Yes, I am, Robert has just dropped me off and is waiting in the car.'

'Oh, is he? Tell him to come in,' Mum suggested.

I ran to the car and told Robert he could wait in the house. However, Robert declined, telling me to send his regards, but he needed to make a phone call.

I went back to the house, got my things ready and then returned to the car. As I climbed into the Toyota Supra, Mum came to the door to see me off. Robert bent forwards, and gave a little wave and grin before driving out of my street.

***

During the two weeks' work experience, I became a little worried because I hadn't learnt anything new, and I had to report back to the school and write about my experience. I could hardly tell them I had been working on the colour of my skin. I was nervous but happy that Mr Field was making an appearance at the modelling agency to take notes and find out how I was getting on. Even though I had nothing to report about the agency throughout the week, I came to life when I spoke about the weekend classes and showed Mr Field my portfolio. He delighted in seeing this.

'Well done, Claire; I am proud,' he said.

'Thank you, sir,' I replied, beaming.

'Mr Field, would you like to come into my office? I'll tell you more about our team and Claire's future here,' Gina asked before gesturing him towards her room.

'Yes, of course, Gina. I have an hour or so before I have to be back at the school,' confirmed Mr Field, who then stood and followed Gina into her office.

Through the door, I could hear chuckles, and I wondered what was being discussed.

Half an hour later, Gina and Mr Field emerged from her room, both smiling.

'I'm going now, Claire,' stated Mr Field, 'It has been great to see what you do here. See you back at school.' He looked at me like a proud dad.

'Bye, sir; see you next week,' I replied. I watched as he walked to the lift with Gina following behind him.

'Enjoy your last few days,' he said, looking over his shoulder.

I smiled; he was my favourite teacher by far.

'Bye Mr Field; it was a pleasure to meet you,' Gina said, holding out her hand, which Mr Field took. She had certainly charmed my teacher, that was for sure!

I sat ruminating about the agency and wondered why Robert had never appeared from his office to say hello to the teacher I had spoken highly about. I was also curious why the phones had barely rung for the last few days of my work experience. Even though Robert blamed it on Elaine leaving and taking many of the professional models with her to another modelling agency, it didn't feel right to question him. I had no reason to doubt what he said and believed his every word.

***

One evening during the autumn of 1992, my uncle excitedly came to my parents' house to show me a newspaper cutting about a competition to win a modelling contract with a top London modelling agency. This sounded promising, but I told him I'd have to ask Northern Teen Models about entering first, because I had a future contract in Japan to look forward to. I called them while he waited.

'Hi Cassandra, it's Claire. Is Gina there, please? I need to speak to her,' I said as I waited nervously for Gina to come on the line.

'Hello Claire, what is it?' she said brightly.

I stumbled to find the right words. 'Er, well, it's just that my uncle has mentioned a competition I could enter to win a contract with a top London modelling agency, and I wanted to ask if it's OK for me to enter?'

Gina's silence made me anxious.

'Oh right, hold the line a minute, Claire,' she said.

I stood by the phone, feeling guilty for asking.

My stomach flipped when Gina said, 'Hi, are you there?' She sounded stern.

'Yes, I am,' I replied wondering what to expect.

'I've just spoken to Robert, and we think you don't need to enter the competition because you already have us an agent, and you'll be going to Japan when you leave school,' Gina stated.

She seemed to be waiting for me to agree, but I was lost for words and felt like I was betraying them for asking.

'Thank you for calling before you entered; this shows your loyalty to us. We'll look forward to seeing you this weekend. Goodnight,' Gina added before ringing off.

I stood facing my uncle and told him, 'They told me I didn't need to enter because they're my agent and I'm going to Japan next year.' I looked into his disappointed face and waited for a response.

'Oh, that's a shame. It looked like a good opportunity to get a modelling agency in London,' he replied.

'Thank you for thinking of me,' I said, and I kissed and hugged him, wondering why I felt like I was making the wrong choice.

***

The Japanese agencies were eager to know when I'd be able to go over there after I left school. Chiyo, the manager from Satu Models in Japan, came over and offered me a good contract if I chose to represent them. Gina promised her I'd take the contract they offered, rather than one of those from the other agencies that were interested. I only had one more year in school, and I couldn't wait for it to be over. Yuki had also been in touch, and had told Gina she would have to come and see me again the following year, or I'd have to go and visit her in London to be remeasured and videoed again, just in case I had changed.

By this time, the only thing that had changed was my name, and this hadn't been discussed with me; it was simply given to me. I was sitting in the office one afternoon when I heard Gina call out, 'Natasha.'

I was puzzled. There were no Natasha's at the agency.

'I'm changing some of your names,' said Gina. 'It's a new start now that I'm head booker. Claire, you'll be called Natasha from now on because there are many Claires and no Natashas'.

I didn't protest and sat repeating Natasha in my head; this felt wrong. I caught sight of my reflection in the mirror – I didn't look like a Natasha – and wondered what my parents would think of the name change. It felt weird telling them, but I was happy they didn't object either. It was only when Gina phoned my house and would ask for Natasha, and my parents would call out, 'Claire,' to get me to come to the phone that it irritated me because I felt like she was disrespecting my parents; however, I was so sucked into their world I couldn't confront them.

***

Gina told us she would be sending a mini book with our pictures in to the various London agencies they were in contact with. If we received a response, we could start working with them, and she would accompany us to visit the agencies in the new year. This puzzled me because I could have entered the competition my uncle excitedly proposed and still had them as an agent.

***

The more time that passed, the more I stayed alone at the house with Robert and Gina on the odd Friday night. Sometimes it felt comfortable and normal, and other times it didn't. I was curious about the other girls' absence; I missed the life and soul of the girls being at the house, and hoped they would be there the next time I stayed. However, I never voiced anything to get answers as to why I had been singled out.

Robert often told me how successful I'd be and that I wouldn't be a 'sexy lady' but a 'foxy lady'. I wondered what he meant by this.

He also added, 'When you reach 16, you'll be at the age of consent, and will be free to do what you want.' Robert said this to the others too, and I found that, as we approached 16, it became more frequent.

I wasn't so naive that I'd think anything other than it was the legal age to have sex.

Robert mentioned age in a way that didn't make me feel uneasy; if anything, he made me feel older by planting the seed in my mind of my coming of age, and the fact that my parents wouldn't have much control over what I did once I reached 16 and left school. Yet, I didn't see that his control and the way he said things wasn't enough for me to approach my family and tell them about discussions at the agency. I was preoccupied most of the time, thinking about my future travels, and I was happy I had Robert and Gina as my surrogate parents, who were satisfying my need for attention.

Gina and I were growing closer. I liked spending time with her; she would pick me up on weekday evenings and take me to aerobics (telling me I needed to keep my body trim for Japan), then drop me home again. She gradually became a best friend because my school friends seemed to have disappeared from my life altogether.

One Friday evening at the models' house, I lay across the living-room floor engrossed in the TV. I still had on my cycling shorts from aerobics, when Gina said casually, 'Natasha, your bum looks like a peach'.

I giggled with embarrassment, turning to face them, and was surprised that I had answered to my new name straight away.

'Yes, it does, Natasha,' Robert said, seeming to get excited, and with a smile that gave me the creeps. 'Cassandra, go and get me a biscuit, then get ready for bed,' he added.

Cassandra did as she was told without objection and was quickly back with a biscuit in her hand. I disliked his demands on people, even though I went along with things too.

'Natasha, would you like Gina to give you a back massage?' he asked.

I turned again to see their smiling faces. 'I'm not bothered; I've never had one before,' I said innocently.

'Gina is good at them. Maybe you could let her try, and if you don't like it, then she can stop,' he suggested.

Gina soon sprang up and knelt down beside me. She started to gently massage my back, before moving to sit over my bum, massaging deeper into my shoulders. I didn't move because it felt OK to experience something I hadn't felt before.

Robert broke the silence and said in a matter-of-fact way, 'When are you 16, Natasha?'

I glanced at him and was a little startled because, as a result of me concentrating on the massage, I hadn't noticed him take his jeans off; he was now lying there in his underpants, covering his crotch with one hand.

'Not until March,' I replied, catching my breath from the deep kneading Gina was giving me. I began to feel uncomfortable and pushed upwards, tensing my shoulders in the hope that she would stop.

She gave my shoulders one last squeeze just as Cassandra entered the room in her bathrobe. I felt weird and embarrassed to be lying on the floor with Gina over the top of me; however, Cassandra didn't seem phased by what she saw.

'Come and sit on the couch, Cassandra. Gina, go up with Natasha and get ready for bed,' said Robert, who then raised his legs for Cassandra to sit down.

I was relieved when Gina released herself from sitting over my body, and I left the living room quickly, wondering what to make of the massage. I had enjoyed it to a point, and – as I wandered to the top floor to get ready for bed – I pondered whether it'd happen again.

Reflection

There were many alarm bells ringing during the events that are described in this chapter. The quiet office, Robert avoiding introducing himself to my mum and my teacher, him commenting that I was a foxy lady rather than a sexy lady, and the changing of my name should have been enough for me to run in a different direction, far away from them. However, having a taste of mature life was very appealing to a young adolescent. I was so focused on my future goal that I wasn't paying full attention to the fine details of the present. Looking at these behaviours together is alarming, but – at the time – they were used subtly throughout the grooming process.

Child molesters can blur the boundaries for years without any violation occurring. The long process of being brainwashed was vital for my abuser to gain my loyalty and avoid me reaching out to others. He also had the help of his girlfriend to make us feel somewhat comfortable and safe. He was able to use her to increase physical contact to desensitise me further. The earlier touch escalated to massage, and this was made to feel normal because she was a woman. Desensitisation is how most sex offenders operate, because this prepares the minor for sexual encounters.

Robert began to create situations for me to be alone with them; this is a typical tactic used by groomers. I was unaware that I was being primed with physical touch. The more time victims spend with their groomers, the more the abusers isolate their victims further. I saw my offenders as parental figures, which overshadowed the perverted behaviours I experienced with them. They had my trust, which gives perpetrators full power. This isn't a position you want to find yourself in, because this leads you to be powerless to do anything and to be a robot to their demands. Whatever relationship you think you have with someone who may be a predator, stop and reflect, because if it's stripping you of your identity, it's not a genuine relationship.

6

THE VIOLATION

I turned 'sweet 16' in the spring of 1993, and I was looking forward to leaving school in the summer. During the May half-term, when I was supposed to be studying for my exams, I stayed at the models' house for the best part of the week.

Also, my father came to visit me at the agency for the first time. I was happy for him to see my place of work, and I waited by the lift to greet him. When he arrived, Gina came out of her office, smiling.

'This is my dad,' I said proudly.

'Hello, it's lovely to meet you,' she said in her most charming way.

I showed him around and I sensed my dad's curiosity as he observed the office atmosphere. I wondered what he was thinking. The office was quiet, but this wasn't unusual.

Robert opened his office door, making me slightly nervous.

'This is my dad,' I said, trying to hide my awkwardness.

Robert approached, holding out his hand; 'Nice to meet you.' Robert seemed unsettled and looked relieved when his phone rang, causing him to leave reception giving his apologies.

My father was long gone when Robert emerged from his

room again. 'Tash, it was good to meet your dad,' he said, lighting a cigarette and rapidly blowing out the smoke to leave a fog between us.

'He is such a lovely man and he is an electrician,' Gina added.

'Thanks,' I said proudly.

'Your father wasn't who I imagined him to be,' stated Robert.

I frowned.

'I mean, I hadn't met him since you joined us, and, because you're sometimes distant towards me, I thought you had been abused by him,' Robert said in a very matter-of-fact manner.

I pictured the look of horror and bewilderment that must have been written across my face. How could he think such a thing and about my father? 'Really?' was all I could muster.

'Now we've met, I can tell this isn't the case,' he added, stubbing out his cigarette. Robert's outrageous allegation was enough for him to change the subject quickly, and he added that he could give my father some electrical work to do at the models' house and asked for my father's availability.

***

On the final day of half-term, Gina and I were sunbathing in the garden. Gina was topless; however, I didn't feel comfortable sunbathing and exposing my breasts.

Robert came out from the house and wiggled happily across the garden. 'Here you go, you two,' he said, handing us drinks.

'You're both turning a lovely colour. Gina, you look like you need sunscreen on. Natasha, why don't you rub some cream into Gina's back?'

Despite the fact I didn't like the way Robert ordered people around, I always found myself being obedient regardless. Robert squeezed some cream onto Gina's back and told me to rub it in. He watched as I shyly smoothed the cream into her skin. Robert's eyes were so focused on the moment that I felt intimidated into stopping.

'Now rub some down her legs,' he urged.

Again, I found myself doing as I was told.

Robert knelt beside me and squeezed cream into his hands. He said, 'This is where she likes to be touched,' and swiftly slipped his hands onto the back of her legs, between her thighs, and sensually massaged towards her crotch. Gina was clearly happy with the attention, moved her body to the rhythm of his hand and let out a giggle.

'Here you do it, Tasha,' Robert said, eagerly taking my hand to repeat what he did.

Only this time, Gina squealed loudly in delight as Robert pressed our hands together on the inside of her upper thigh.

'Look she enjoys that!' Robert breathed in a twisted voice, clearly excited with the situation he was creating.

I felt cornered and unable to get away from the situation, even if I had tried. The only thing I was able to do was laugh the experience off, although it left me confused, as I knew deep down that this wasn't right.

***

In June, I sat my exams half-heartedly, knowing my future didn't lie in the academic world. My last day at school was a whirlwind of chaos, with all of Year 11 running round excitedly signing shirts and others embracing tearfully to say goodbye. I observed my surroundings and the people I had spent the last five years with; it was strange to think life wouldn't be a school routine any more. I left the gates for the last time with Jamie, with whom I'd walked home from school for years. We strolled along the familiar streets, chatting about the memories we shared, until we turned into his road eventually and hugged goodbye.

I walked away, feeling a stab of sadness and wondering if I'd see him again, or any of the others, for that matter. I felt lonely when it suddenly dawned on me that maybe I wouldn't bump into anyone because I was heading on a different path, which didn't involve my old friends. It was the new ones I was welcoming, as they held the power that would make my dreams into reality. I mentally said goodbye to the old path, and walked towards my new one, now that I was free from school. This new journey was about to fully flourish in ways I couldn't have imagined.

***

The moment I left school, Gina inserted herself more into my daily life. She drove me to pick up my exam results, and – even though my grades were poor – I was pleased to share them with someone. Her non-judgemental response and praise for trying my best made me feel better. I stood in the adult world with Gina and Robert firmly at my side, and a taste of the high life became a frequent experience for me and the other chosen girls. We were driven around the UK, introduced to wealthy businessmen and told they could help with our careers. We would excitedly get ready in the clothes Gina loaned us, and Robert served us drinks before meeting them. During the dinners, his friends asked about our futures and where we might be heading, before adding that they could be of assistance in some way.

Dale was in his 50s; he seemed very powerful in his fancy suits and he flashed his wealth by saying we could order anything we wanted. He owned many things, and told us about his glossy magazine, which he said we could do a photoshoot for. This sounded exciting to budding models just starting out. (However, we were never paid for it.) Being naive and impressionable, after a few drinks I found myself flirting with these men with the others. Robert seemed to love creating situations like this, and would sit back and watch us with his beady eyes.

It didn't take long for the photoshoot to be organised. They paid for our hair to be cut at a top salon and for us to go on sunbeds. In the Manchester hotel suite, Gina applied our make-up. The room was beautifully old fashioned; I had never set foot in a such a fancy hotel before.

Dale arrived at the shoot with the photographer for his magazine, and he sat behind the lighting to watch. Robert came and went from the room, passing Dale drinks; he seemed to be at Dale's beck and call. This was the only time I witnessed Robert serve someone and didn't see him as the all-powerful, dominating figure he usually was. It was now Dale who girls were introduced to frequently.

For the photoshoot, we all had to do the same pose on the bed. We wore black, fitted minidresses, and were asked to lie down, raise our legs up the wall from the bed frame and look back towards the camera. Dale was clearly delighted as he watched the photoshoot, and he said how great we looked.

After the photoshoot, we were taken out for dinner. I found Dale to be somewhat creepy, but this was veiled with charm. He listened while I spoke about Japan, and interjected that I had a bright future ahead.

On other occasions, Robert drove us to his friend's radio station and then on to his nightclub. The girls and I had fun dancing, as Gina, Robert and his rich friend looked down from the second level that overlooked the dance floor. Robert asked us to do our routines from the classes, and I cringed because we did what was asked. I could tell from the club goers' expressions that they were wondering what was happening on the dance floor. It was like we were to put on show for the world to see, only it was just for the benefit of Robert and his friends. (We didn't pay for anything while we were with Robert, life felt like a free ride, but this ride I was on would have its repercussions later.)

***

During this time when I was staying at the models' house, I never got paid for working at the modelling agency any more and often wondered why. However, from time to time, Robert gave me pocket money, which I was thankful for. It was like he was drip feeding me to keep me hanging on for more.

Mum was called into the modelling agency to sign a paper stating that I couldn't leave it or home, but if I did leave home, I'd move from there to the models' house. Before signing, Mum told Robert she wouldn't tell me what to do and if I chose to leave then I could. Robert seemed unnerved by this, but went along with what Mum said.

Before leaving, Mum and Robert had a conversation about the condition of her back. Robert was quick to offer support, and said he would pick Mum up on her day off from work, and he or Gina would take her to have some physiotherapy, which he would pay for. This kindness pleased me and made me grateful to have him in my life.

***

Most of us were 16, and our parents had already given permission for us to have alcohol, so it became a regular occurrence at the last Saturday class for Robert to send brandy and Coke in for the girls staying at the house. By the time the class ended, we would be a little tipsy and under the watchful eye of the sober girls, who looked on curiously.

During dinner, we were fuelled with more alcohol, which made us livelier than we already were, having known each other for a few years by then. Robert seemed to enjoy this spirited banter. However, the laughter changed to nervous giggles when he turned the chit-chatting into a game of guessing who had a boyfriend and who was still a virgin. Although, he initiated the conversation, he sat back and listened as we told each other snippets of our encounters with boys.

Robert intervened, saying, 'Cassandra, what do you think about Natasha?' He paused before carrying on. 'You probably have, knowing where you live,' he added with a watchful eye.

I hated being in the hot seat and wasn't sure what to say. Robert made me feel embarrassed about my virginity remaining intact, yet – on the other hand – I felt smug, as he couldn't be further away from the truth in what he thought.

Robert turned to Cassandra. 'I'm sure she isn't a virgin,' he said, searching her face for an answer.

'I think she is,' Cassandra replied knowingly.

I couldn't bring myself to say anything and was grateful for the food arriving at the table to derail the conversation, so nothing more could be said.

***

During the autumn of 1993, the models' house was becoming like my second home. My father came to do some work on the house, and I was proud to show him round, repeating the same tour I'd received from Gina. Dad wasn't one to comment, but made his observations while Gina and Robert showed their hospitality, and I was happy to show Robert that my father was a good man.

Life had changed so much from when I was hanging out on the streets of Manchester to becoming a professional model who was about to travel half way across the world for work. Gina and I were almost inseparable; I was like a puppy following and shadowing her every move. Also, the bedroom arrangements had changed at the models' house, and I found myself sleeping in Robert and Gina's room. I wondered about this change, because I had slept in the top bedroom for so long. Again, I stayed mute and was unable to voice my curiosity as to why I was now sleeping in the single bed next to them. I seemed to have been pushed into their room because the occasional new girl who stayed was given the top-floor bedroom. In some ways, I didn't want to displease Gina and Robert by protesting, because I had grown fond of them, and these emotions made me feel powerless to tell them I was uncomfortable with the change.

Even when Gina became more touchy-feely, and started to cuddle and caress me, I found myself willingly going along with what she wanted to do. It felt strange being with a woman who was more than a decade older, and I didn't know what to do when Gina's advances came on more strongly; it was like I was unable to challenge her. Although I liked to be touched in such a loving and gentle way, it was weird that a woman was showing me this intimate affection. I wanted to be able to express to someone what I was experiencing and ask whether what she was doing was normal. But my inner questioning couldn't be answered, because my voice had become stunted. I certainly couldn't approach my parents with the things that happened at the models' house, because I feared they would put an end to me attending the agency, which would stop me from reaching my goals. (I had fallen knee deep into this lifestyle, to the point of no return.)

In my naivety, I couldn't see any badness or that I was trapped in some perverted family triangle with them. I yearned for the attention of my parents, who were there in many ways but not in others, and Robert and Gina used this knowledge to their advantage by building my self-esteem and giving me advice to build up my confidence for Asia. I was always enthusiastic about this topic, because it would send me into a world of my own, so I wasn't fully concentrating on my present experiences. They led me, like the parents I craved for reassurance and guidance, while bringing me even closer to them than before, and I didn't know I was being used as a pawn in their warped game. I believed that, without their influence, my modelling career in Japan wouldn't become a reality.

Gina's advances soon changed from caressing and cuddling into kissing. It was weird kissing a woman; her lips were gentle and thinner than the firmness of a man's, and I wasn't sure if I liked it. Yet, I acquiesced to her every move. Gina and Robert had me securely under the evil spell they had cast, and – whatever they commanded – I surrendered to the flow with whatever Gina wanted to do. However, this confused me about my sexuality and who I was in relation to my potential future partner. Up to this point, I had been only interested in boys and still preferred them, even though I was experiencing this with a female. I knew Robert was in the distance, controlling all situations, and that he was behind the advances Gina made towards me. And, since I liked her more than Robert, I let her touch me in places only Sean had touched.

Many times, I became irritated at their controlling ways. Robert told everyone what to do, when we would eat, what we ate, who slept where and which girls got ready for bed first. And he ordered each of us not to wear underwear for bed, because it was the house rules, and he told us it was disgusting and very unhygienic. Sometimes I wanted to stand up to Robert and Gina, and scream at them. Why should I do as I was told by them when my own parents didn't tell me what to do, what to eat or when to go to bed? And my own mother didn't tell me off if I wore knickers for bed.

Even though I sensed something wasn't quite right, I thought it best not to approach anyone. After all, once I started travelling, I'd see less of Robert and Gina. And so I carried on, happy in the knowledge that in less than five months I'd be on a plane to Tokyo.

***

The nights were drawing in, and one Saturday we sat waiting for our orders from Robert after the Saturday classes; he had been in his office for some time. I still wondered what he did in there most days, and it niggled me when he made himself scarce if there were any outside visitors. Robert finally opened his door, with a cigarette hanging from his mouth. He took a drag and flicked the ash, missing the ashtray, and then said, 'OK, girls, you may go to the cinema this evening, but go for dinner first.'

Our faces lit up. As I jumped up from where I sat to gather my belongings, Robert stopped me.

He said, 'Natasha, you'll stay here and help Gina call the girls to make sure they're attending the classes tomorrow.' He casually stubbed out his cigarette in the ashtray before returning to his office. Releasing my grip from my bag, I looked over at Karen.

She put the palms of her hands up and shrugged her shoulders. This was something new; no one had stayed behind before, apart from Cassandra the odd time. Emotions washed over me; I didn't like being the favourite any more, especially now when it was interfering with the fun I'd have with the girls.

Robert emerged from his office with cash and walked towards Cassandra, saying, 'Here, Cassandra, you be the banker. Go to the Dutch Pancake House for dinner, then choose something you all want to see at the cinema.' He placed the money in her hand and squeezed it, smiling sweetly into her face.

'Thank you, Robert, you are kind.' Cassandra kissed him on the cheek and glanced at me.

I wasn't sure what to make of the look in her eyes and the affection shared between them, which Gina didn't seem to be bothered about even though she and Robert were a couple.

'Thank you,' Karen added.

One by one, the girls thanked Robert as they tumbled into the lift or down the stairs, laughing as they went. He seemed empowered by this adoration. I sat, feeling deflated, as I watched Robert go back into his office, but this time he left his door open. From where I was sitting, I could make out that the draped curtain was open. I moved slightly in my chair and willed my eyes to see round the corner, but jumped back when Robert pushed a black bag underneath the curtain. However, I was more bothered about having to sit in the office with them all evening, waiting for the girls to return.

How dare he spoil my fun and keep me from hanging out with them, I thought.

'Are you OK, Natasha?' Gina asked gently.

'Yes, I'm fine,' I replied and wondered why I said yes, when clearly I wasn't happy with the situation.

'Here, you do this list of girls; we'll get through them in no time,' Gina added passing me a list and sitting at the desk beside me.

I surprised myself as I enjoyed phoning the girls to ask if they were OK and would be attending classes the following day. I knew some of them looked up to me because I had taught them what I knew.

Robert stood at his door, with a bright smile, and asked, 'How are you both getting on?'

'Nearly done here,' Gina said looking up sweetly.

'I've poured you both brandies,' he said, briefly going out of sight to get the drinks from his office.

My eyes followed him as he headed towards us; he seemed cheerful about something. He smiled, handing me the brandy and Coke.

'Thanks,' I replied, my voice sounding pissed off that I had to stay behind. I looked at my drink and wondered what the white froth was inside the top half of the glass.

'Drink that; it has been a busy day for you,' commanded Robert, as he shot a look at Gina; they were speaking, but without words. He walked casually into the catwalk room with that funny little shuffle, which I was beginning to find off putting, and I had an urge to trip him up.

'Cheers, Natasha,' Gina said, raising her glass to take a sip.

I noticed her glass didn't have the white froth at the top. 'Cheers,' I replied, taking a sip. I grimaced because it was stronger than normal. I placed the glass on the table and noticed that the froth didn't melt away when the fizz settled from the Coke. It was as if something had been put in it and was unable to dissolve fully. I turned my attention to what Robert was doing in the next room; it sounded like he was dragging furniture around, and I heard the opening and closing of the filing cabinet. When I had finished calling the last of the girls, I felt flushed from the brandy and wondered what I'd be doing next.

Robert appeared from the catwalk room and said, 'The back room is ready, Gina; I'll be out for a couple of hours.'

I sat there feeling bemused by what he meant.

Robert slipped back into his office closing the door, only to reappear moments later with his coat, wallet and two more brandies.

'See you later,' Gina said, as Robert left the office looking satisfied.

The first sip wasn't so bad; it actually gave me a rushing and warming sensation round my body that I hadn't had before. It was strange, but felt good.

Gina asked me to follow her to the back room when we finished our drinks; I was happy to do so because of my curiosity about the noise Robert had made. I felt weird wandering into the catwalk room, which remained unchanged. Gina opened the mirrored door, and I was taken aback to find the floor covered with blankets and pillows facing the mirrors, and a tub of moisturising cream placed at the side. I looked up to face Gina, who sat on the windowsill looking provocative; I didn't know what to make of it all. Gina slowly began to take her clothes off, I stood there staring at her and wondered what situation I had got myself into.

'Take your clothes off, and I'll give you a massage,' Gina said, now stripped to her underwear.

I was stunned as Gina moved a few steps towards me and began to help me undress.

'Lie down, and I'll give you a full body massage,' she said guiding me to the floor.

I quickly lay on my front.

Gina undid my bra strap, took some cream into her hands and rubbed it into my back, 'How does that feel, Tasha?' Gina asked, with her voice low and husky.

'It's nice,' I replied, already being accustomed to her good back massages.

As I felt the brandy wash over me, Gina gently started massaging my bum and inner thighs, which sent sensations across my body, and strong rushes in my stomach and genitals. I was conflicted because I was in a terrifying situation, yet my body didn't feel like my own. Gina's massages were always the same, but this one felt different because my body tingled at her touch, my head started to spin and everything was slightly hazy.

'Turn over, Tasha,' Gina breathed.

I turned and watched Gina release her bra, and I froze facing her hard nipples. *This isn't right,* I thought, but I lay there helpless, wondering what she would do next.

Gina took more cream from the tub and rubbed it into her hands, before confidently placing her hands over my tummy and firmly massaging the cream up towards my breasts and nipples. I was shocked because my personal space was being invaded. Gina was overstepping the boundaries without asking if she could arouse my sexuality. I felt trapped and looked horror-struck into her face as she knelt over me. I was stuck in time, even though my body became aroused by her caressing round my breasts.

My mind was in a state of bewilderment with questions filling my mental space. I was too petrified to get up, because where would I run to? Should I get dressed and stay in reception? Or run home and face questioning from my parents, who would wonder why I was back from the house at such a late hour on a Saturday night? My body didn't feel like my own, and these overwhelming feelings made my stomach and chest churn, and my heart rate increase. I was thirsty, not knowing if I wanted brandy or a glass of water, while Gina carried on massaging my front.

She looked into my eyes then manoeuvred to pull my knickers down. I'd never been fully naked with her before, and I felt vulnerable when she spread my legs apart, making me feel exposed and anxious. She then put her head between my legs and licked my genitals, while pressing my lower tummy with her hand. There was no doubt she had done this before. I was dazed and confused, and tried to stiffen my body, but I had poor muscle control, and was too relaxed for my mind to take over and tell her this shouldn't be happening. I lay there wide-eyed, looking at the ceiling and knowing full well she was doing something terribly wrong, but the stirrings of arousal took over from the way she was using me to gratify herself. No one had taken me with their mouth before. I closed my eyes and thought of Sean, having not got this far with him. How I wished it was Sean and not a woman going down on me. I began to feel uncomfortable because she spent a lot of time between my legs. I wanted her to stop, because it was sinful, but the feelings rushing round my body made me helpless.

Gina began to slow down and lay next to me to smiling. 'How was that, Natasha?' she asked in a ravenous voice.

I hesitated, then said, 'It was good,' my voice cracking from dryness.

Gina lowered her face for a kiss. I winced because she had just gone down on me, and I didn't want to taste her breath. She gently took my hand and placed it on her genitals; she was wet.

I didn't like feeling her hairy genitals on my fingers, but I wasn't able to remove them because she kept her hand on top of mine and used force to become aroused by her own movement. It felt like I wasn't there as she pressed deeper into herself, not letting go of my hand, and she began to breathe heavily, pushing her fingers inside herself and releasing mine.

I looked into the mirror and didn't like what was happening. This wasn't what I envisioned for my future. I remained lying in the same position; I was thrown and didn't know what to do.

Gina was intense and carried on playing with herself, then lay on top of me and began circling her lower body, trying to get some feeling from our pelvises rubbing together. This didn't feel normal, and I flinched at the pain of our bones digging into each other. My mind was shouting, *Get off me*, but I stayed motionless underneath her, knowing it wasn't right that I remained with a woman who was forcing herself onto me. She carried on, clearly enjoying what she was doing. She sat up to reach her climax and I jumped when I heard the lift doors open.

'It's OK, it's only Robert,' she said.

'Oh,' was all I could manage, feeling stifled, while thinking, *Get me out of here.*

'We can just stay here for a while, before going back to reception,' she tried to arouse me further, but I stiffened wanting her to stop. My genitals began to hurt with more force she used. I thought of the girls being back at any moment, and sadness washed over me that I was in this state. I wanted to burst into tears – how did it get this far?

As I dressed, I blinked, thinking it was some dream that would be over soon, but the sad realisation was real. Walking through reception, I felt embarrassed and held my head down in shame. Robert didn't say anything as I walked to the washroom.

I sat on the toilet taking deep breaths; my pubic bone hurt and I wondered why my wee was taking so long when I was bursting to go. I looked up to the ceiling, breathing in the cool air and asked myself what the hell I was doing. I felt like I needed to throw up whatever was stuck in my chest.

'Are you OK in there, Natasha?' Gina said, tapping lightly on the door, which made me jump.

'Yes, I'll be out in a minute,' I replied. I wondered how long I had been sitting on the toilet for.

'Would you like a drink?' she added.

'Yes, water,' I answered, still willing my pee to make its arrival.

I looked in the mirror, and was startled by my flushed cheeks and dilated pupils. I felt paranoid and threw some water over my face to try to wash away what had happened, but to no avail. I wandered back to reception and wasn't able to look them in the eye. They sat chit-chatting as if everything was normal, while I was trying to think clearly. My body seemed like it was on some come down from a strange high.

I felt on edge as I heard the lift ascend to bring the girls to the office. I tried to sit normally, like nothing had happened, but I was sure the girls could tell what I'd been up to because of my rosy cheeks. I was ashamed at the thought of them ever finding out, yet somehow it seemed as though Cassandra knew, because she was studying my face intently, and my flushed face was showing no signs of settling down. I felt alien, like a part of me had faded away from the group. They were lively as they spoke of their eventful evening, and I sat listening and wishing I'd been with them, rather than thinking about the last hour during which my body had been used for Gina's sexual gratification. (I believe my drink was laced with a form of ecstasy because, years later, I tried a substance that gave me similar sensations in my body to those I experienced back then.)

Robert knew I was infatuated with Gina and wanted to be like her. However, the conflict I was experiencing confused me, now that I'd stepped into the realm of sexual contact and exploring my sexuality. For the first time, I began to feel frightened by who I was and why I had allowed Gina to use me in a sexual way. I wondered if it'd happen again and, without any protest, I knew I wouldn't be the instigator because it didn't feel normal. I started feeling sorry for myself, because I didn't have my old school friends to reach out to, and I couldn't tell the girls because I was scared by what Robert's reaction would be if I spoke of this dirty little secret. I felt alone as we left the modelling agency, everything was in slow motion, the girls were just an echo in the background of my mind, and Gina and Robert looked cosy and content in their coupled world.

Reflection

Before the violation occurred, Robert made sure to deceive my parents by showing kindness and hospitality, because he needed to throw them off the scent of his hidden agenda. I was at the age of consent and no longer seen as a child in the eyes of the law, which meant 16-year-olds were fair game to Robert. Like many offenders, Robert and Gina slotted themselves frequently into my daily life when I left school. Groomers approach their victims differently and behave in age-appropriate ways. With a child, they'll play games or toy fight, and because I was a teenager my abuser diverted conversations to intimate disclosures about boyfriends and sexual matters; this was made to feel normal because we were revealing secrets in a peer group. These are not conversations you should have with someone you see as a mentor; this is someone who is blurring the boundaries to control and manipulate you into participating in sexual encounters.

Robert also pushed us towards his inner circle of wealthy business friends, which was to coerce us into having sex with them at some point. Back then, I couldn't tell that they were perverted old men manipulating and steering us into a world where they could take advantage of our innocent youth. This is similar to trafficking, where young people become victims in the buying and selling of sexual services, as predators look to network with other paedophiles.

When it has got to the stage of the sexual violation occurring, you're in a state of not knowing what to do. I was at an awkward age when I should have known better, but I was confused by the situation and thought no one would believe me if I told them what I'd experienced, since it looked like I was a willing participant. I knew it was wrong, yet I was unable to see them for what they were, because I was emotionally attached to them. However, this was (and is) the result of the calculated grooming process.

7

LIVING THE DREAM

Gina organised photoshoots for the group. I needed extra test pictures to make my portfolio stronger, as this would give me a better chance of obtaining work in Japan the following year. I was excited to be shooting with a new photographer, because I had outgrown Danny and wanted something different in my book. I became more relaxed in front of the camera and was able to take my first Polaroid picture to start a photo collage in the back of my book. At the beginning of my modelling journey, I had admired the Polaroids in models' books and had longed for the day I'd receive mine. Doing something so small pleased me. As I placed the Polaroid in my portfolio, I stared at myself in the long, cream, satin nightdress Gina had loaned me for the photoshoot; I looked so much older than 16. It was hard to imagine myself as the baggy-clothed, tracksuit-wearing girl from Longsight who had been transformed into looking glamorous in print.

***

The modelling agency received a call for a casting for a bridal magazine, and Gina was eager for me to get the job. She told me that if I got it, it'd be a good experience and the beginning of building my portfolio with tear sheets.

I wore Gina's clothes for the casting, and she drove me to the studio in Ardwick Green. I felt more confident due to having new pictures and Gina by my side to promote me. Luckily, Gina had known the photographer, Mike, for many years.

When we arrived, Gina greeted Mike, saying, 'Hi Mike, it's great to see you. You look well; how are you?' Gina was on form with her charm.

'Hi Gina, it's good to see you; I'm well, thanks,' replied Mike.

They kissed each other on both cheeks, and talked for a while about the changes at the modelling agency, and how she was building up the new-faces section and starting from scratch, since most of the older models had left. We sat, and I placed my book on the table in front of them.

'Anyway, Mike, this is Natasha. She left school this year and is beginning to model full time; she is going to Japan next January,' Gina said passing Mike my portfolio.

'Wow, Japan; that's a great opportunity, Natasha,' he exclaimed and began flicking through my pictures. He scrutinised my face, making me feel uncomfortable due to not knowing what he was thinking.

'I'm sure she would be good for what you're looking for, Mike,' Gina added breaking the silence.

'We're seeing a lot of people today, and there are a few models we're interested in who will be coming from London to be cast. I'll keep Natasha in mind and check what the clients think, as she may be too young for what we need,' Mike responded, and he had one last flick through my book before passing it back.

I was embarrassed, as I was standing at the entrance door, and waiting for Mike and Gina to finish their private conversation. It was like he was only taking an interest because Gina desperately wanted me to get the job.

After the meeting ended, we got back in Gina's car for the trip back. In the car, Gina said, 'I reckon he'll consider you and push you forwards when he talks with the clients later.' She smiled while she was reversing the car.

'Thank you, Gina, for coming with me. I don't think I'd have been able to sell myself and got anywhere,' I replied.

Gina squeezed my hand and stated, 'It's my job, and I really want you to be chosen, so you can have some work experience before you travel next year.'

I stayed silent on the way back to the modelling agency.

***

A few days later, Mike phoned with the news that I'd be a bridesmaid in the bridal brochure. I was surprised, because I had resigned myself to the fact that there had been too many girls to cast and so I thought I wouldn't even be considered. I had a lot to thank Gina for; if it wasn't for her persistence, then I wouldn't be excited about being booked for my first photoshoot on location.

***

Two weeks later, on the first day of the shoot, I was up early and feeling happy. I hadn't needed to spend the night in their room and had woken up in the top bedroom to a tranquil atmosphere. The night before, Robert had suggested I slept alone to get a good night's rest ahead of the shoot. I had leapt from my chair and up the stairs, past Robert's bedroom, feeling elated that I was out of the prison confines of their bedroom.

A little later that morning, Gina drove me to Mike's studio. When we arrived, Gina said, 'Good luck, Natasha,' reached over to give me a hug and tried to kiss me at the same time.

I let her give me a kiss on the cheek and hoped she wouldn't get out of the car to say hello; she was like an embarrassing mother at times.

'Thanks for dropping me off,' I replied, gathering my bags quickly.

Gina squeezed my hand. 'Goodbye, I'll see you in five days. I'll be here to pick you up,' she said, smiling.

'I'm near home, so I can jump on the bus when I get back and go to stay with my parents. I haven't seen them for a while,' I explained as I eagerly stepped from the car and looked forward to having some freedom.

'OK, call me when you arrive at the location, to let us know you've settled in,' Gina confirmed, and with that she drove off, waving, while I breathed a sigh of relief.

Gina could be intense, and she suffocated me at times; she was overbearing with her advances of affection, especially in public. However, I noticed she wouldn't show affection to me in front of Robert, which was fine as I was confused about my emotions. I was feeling weird about them being a couple and me being her 'bit on the side.'

Opening the doors to the studio, I met Mike's assistants, with whom I was to travel. They were two young men in their 20s, and my stomach fluttered when one approached and introduced himself.

'Hi, I'm Joe; it's nice to meet you,' he said, holding out his hand.

I hesitated to meet it with my clammy hand. 'Hi, I'm Claire – oh, Natasha, I mean – that's my model name.'

Joe looked puzzled, 'Shall I call you Natasha then?' he said, releasing his firm grip.

'Yes, I guess so,' I replied. My cheeks flushed, and I didn't know if it was from his attractive features, or from my mistake in giving my real name and feeling a fool for doing so.

***

I barely spoke a word in the van as we travelled to Lincolnshire. I was sitting so close to Joe that our arms brushed together from time to time as we drove down country lanes. His handsome, blond looks and muscular physique made me shy. And his voice rang through my ears as he spoke to the other assistant, whose name I'd forgotten. They tried to get me to join in the conversation by asking questions about modelling, but I felt like a silly, immature girl because I hadn't lived long enough to even begin to have an in-depth discussion about life experiences, particularly with someone I now fancied. I daydreamed about my strong desire to have him, and it suddenly dawned on me that I hadn't been in close proximity to any males since Sean.

***

Eventually, we reached our destination. The country manor house was a beautiful sight as we drove up the winding road towards its main entrance. I had never been to such a place; I had only admired country-estate homes in magazines.

When we pulled up, Mike walked up to the van; he was keen to open the back doors so he could retrieve his camera equipment. I was happy to jump out and get away from the intense feelings I was having towards Joe.

'Hi Natasha, how are you?' Mike said.

'I'm fine, thank you,' I replied, not knowing what else to say, but relieved to have some fresh air.

'How was the journey, Joe?' Mike added, opening the van doors.

'It was a good drive, as there wasn't a lot of traffic about,' confirmed Joe, before helping Mike unload.

I stood watching Joe; his arms were toned and I imagined him pulling me close for a passionate kiss. I tried to shake away the thoughts I was having, because I felt my cheeks blush.

'Let's get the equipment into the house and do a recce round the estate. Natasha, this is Michelle, the make-up artist,' explained Mike.

I hadn't noticed Michelle approach the van.

'It's lovely to meet you, Natasha; let's go in and get a warm drink,' Michelle said.

'OK, I just need to grab my bag,' I replied.

'Hi Joe, how are you? It's great to see you,' she continued. Michelle's tone of voice was alluring.

I frowned and grabbed my bags, not wanting to hear the exchanges between them – they clearly knew each other well. I didn't like the jealously I was feeling as I followed Michelle to the house and into the kitchen.

'How long have you been modelling for, Natasha?' Michelle queried, putting the kettle on.

'I've been with the modelling agency for over two years—' I began.

'Have you had much work?' Michelle interrupted.

'No, this is my first job. I've been on castings and just had test shoots,' I replied, feeling small.

'Congratulations on getting your first job. Mike is great to work with, and you'll receive some nice photos for your portfolio.' Michelle beamed.

'Thanks,' I said, smiling back; I couldn't help but like her for making me feel at ease with her bubbly personality.

'Natasha, would you mind if I tweezed your eyebrows for this photoshoot?' Michelle studied my face. 'They'll look good reshaped. Come on, let's take our drinks to my room.' She picked up the teas and nodded with her head for me to follow her.

'OK,' I agreed; I could hardly protest on my first job.

I followed her out of the kitchen, through the house and, eventually, into her room.

'Sit down, Natasha,' she said, 'I just need to find my tweezers. I haven't had time to unpack everything yet.'

I looked around the messy room and found a seat by the dressing table, which was covered with make-up bags.

'Over the next few days, after breakfast, you'll probably come to me and have your make-up done first,' Michelle added, looking through various bags.

'Here they are,' she exclaimed, 'Let's shape these eyebrows. I can tell they've never been touched, so this may hurt a little.' Michelle started to tweeze and pull the excess hairs from my brows.

I wanted to scream out in pain – 'a little,' she had said! Tears stung my eyelids.

'Are you OK, Natasha?' Michelle said softly.

'Er, yes,' I managed to muster.

'I'm nearly done. The redness will fade, but look how your face has changed already,' she explained.

I winced and looked in the mirror, only noticing that my skin was reddened from the pain.

After that, we sat on her bed for a while, watching TV and chit-chatting. I noticed how stiff I became as I sat next to her.

Flashbacks from Gina beginning to stroke me and ask questions about my personal life washed over me, and I began to feel paranoid that Michelle might start making advances towards me. I was relieved when the lady of the house knocked on the door to say my room was ready.

I followed her to the attic, which overlooked the vast back garden in the grounds of the house. The view pleased me, and I gazed from the window, experiencing a sense of freedom at being away from Robert and Gina.

'Natasha,' a voice called faintly up the stairs, shortly followed by, 'Are you there?' as Michelle tapped on the door.

'Yes, sorry, I was in my own world and just unpacking,' I replied, opening the door to Michelle's jolly face.

'Mike needs you; he wants to take some pictures and work out how the bridal brochure will be set out. It'll save some time tomorrow before the models from London arrive,' she confirmed.

I was nervous and daunted by the prospect of shooting side by side with professional models from the south. I was sure my inexperience would show somehow.

***

A short time later, I followed Mike round the idyllic grounds; I was a city girl, but was able to appreciate the beautiful countryside surrounding me. Mike stood me in different spots while he took Polaroids.

Finally, he said, 'I think we're done for today, Natasha. We'll be shooting at a bigger estate house the day after tomorrow. For now, let's go and have dinner; you must be hungry too.'

His genuine warmth made me feel safe. This job was the

beginning of living the model-life dream; I was being paid for a photoshoot and being taken out for dinner without having to put a hand in my purse. And I was able to see beautiful parts of England that I wouldn't otherwise experience.

***

We soon went to dinner. I sat at the end of the dining table listening to the chatter, and again I reflected on my 16 years of life and wished I had things to share in the conversations.

'Natasha, Gina said you're going to Japan,' Mike exclaimed, looking across the table.

It appeared I was in the hot seat because everyone turned to face me. 'Yes, I go in January for two months,' I stated. I waited for the next question, not sure how to elaborate.

'Will you be travelling with anyone else?' Mike asked.

'No, no one can go at that time, but they said I'll be sharing an apartment with other girls when I arrive,' I replied. I took a sip of water because my nerves had made my mouth dry.

'You're so young, but brave to be going out there on your own,' Mike said as he looked at the clients for confirmation of his statement. 'I mean, I don't think I'd let my daughter go alone at such a young age; are your parents OK with you going?' Mike added.

I felt under interrogation as I answered, 'Yes, they're OK about me going. By January, I'll be nearly 17.' I smiled, willing the conversation to be steered in another direction.

As the chatter changed towards a different subject, I sat there questioning who I was and wondered if I was too young to go away without my parents. Also, my new name seemed weird and it was confusing that everyone was calling me Natasha.

I felt like two people in the same body and that I could hide behind either one at any time. I was Natasha in the modelling world and Claire in my inner world.

***

That night, I fell into bed and lay for a while listening to the night-time breeze hit the window; it was so peaceful. In the stillness, I had space to think and hear my mind's chatter, rather than being in a room hearing two people whose night-time rituals unsettled me, but who had immobilised me from saying so. Robert was always last to get into bed; he would potter around in his underpants before getting into bed beside Gina. It was like he wanted to show off his manly physique in the hope I'd be attracted to him somehow, then Gina would snuggle up to him as he read his book or he would tell us to go to sleep while he carried on reading. However, I couldn't sleep with the light on. Occasionally, Gina would turn over and search for my hand to hold. Sometimes I'd offer mine, or roll over and face the wall, wondering why I was like a robot in letting them control most of my moves. They felt like my parents, only my parents wouldn't treat me this way. With these floating thoughts, I finally drifted off to sleep, happy that I was alone.

***

I woke up feeling refreshed, opened the window and breathed in the crisp air. The morning dew made the air moist, and the smell of the freshly cut grass hit my nose, making me sneeze. I stood by the window, looking at the grounds, and dreamt of owning a home like this one day, with children running around. I was present and aware of dreaming about a clear future, which didn't involve Gina or Robert.

A little while later, I met everyone for breakfast in the quaint cottage kitchen.

'Good morning, Natasha, did you sleep well?' Michelle asked.

'Yes, I did, thanks; the attic is really peaceful,' I confirmed. I sat down, admiring Michelle's confidence. It felt very homely with everyone helping themselves to the prepared food on the table, and Mike was by the grill, turning bacon, before sitting down to make a sandwich.

'We'll begin with you, Natasha, as the other models are stuck in traffic and won't be here until later this afternoon,' Mike said and then he turned to Michelle. 'Michelle, start with Natasha's make-up after breakfast. We need her to look old enough to be a bride today.' Mike left the kitchen with Joe to begin setting up.

I felt a little pressured and hoped I could carry off a bridal dress, even though I looked so young.

'Natasha, when you've finished breakfast, come up to my room and we'll get going' Michelle added, leaving the kitchen.

***

I sat silently in Michelle's room while she chatted away and applied my make-up. From time to time, I caught a glimpse of myself in the mirror and was amazed at how much my face had changed since having my eyebrows plucked into a womanly shape.

I was a little anxious when we were called to begin the shoot. I was helped into different dresses, before the client chose a Bo Peep style gown in shantung, with a ruched shawl collar. Even though it was weird to be wearing a wedding dress so young, I felt like a wealthy lady of the manor walking round the grounds.

I had forgotten about home until I was told to take a call in the kitchen.

The client passed me the phone and said, 'It's your booker.' She nodded and walked away.

'Hello,' I said faintly.

'Hi Natasha, you didn't call us,' Gina retorted.

'Oh, I forgot,' I replied, feeling awkward.

'How is the shoot?' Gina asked.

'It's good; I'm being shot in some of the bridal dresses,' I said quickly, wanting to get off the phone because I was annoyed at Gina interrupting my work. It seemed like I couldn't get away from them, no matter where I was.

'That's great, Tasha. I knew you'd make a good impression with the clients and Mike. I can't wait to see you; I'm missing you!' Gina exclaimed.

'Yes, you too,' I said, yet I didn't feel the same. I agreed out of a sense of duty because Gina had got me the job, and – now I felt indebted to her – I could hardly say I wasn't missing her and Robert, or the models' house, for that matter. I feared they would be annoyed with my lack of consideration for them while I was away.

***

The five days flew by. I didn't want the shoot to end because it meant not seeing Joe every day. However, I was excited about returning to see my parents and having them say they were proud of me, and also that I'd put some work Polaroids in the back of my book. I had learnt many things from the photoshoot, and was happy my feet were firmly on the road to becoming a professional in the industry. It was uncanny that my first assignment was a bridal shoot, because now I had been confirmed to be a model by being a bride and getting married to the job.

I came back to the city of Manchester with a boost of confidence from the job. Gina picked me up from the studio and, as we headed to the main road in Ardwick, she drove round the roundabout into town.

'Oh, I thought I was going to be taken home to my family? I can't wait to see them,' I said watching the turn for Longsight disappear out of sight.

'Are your parents in?' Gina asked.

I had to think for a moment. 'No, they're at work, but will be home later,' I replied. Many times, I missed not being with my family, and this was a time when I was full of excitement and wanted to tell them about my first assignment.

'Maybe I could drop you off later, if you want?' Gina said, turning the car into the streets of the city centre.

'OK,' I replied reluctantly. I chatted about the shoot all the way back to the house; I had moved in without really knowing what was happening to my freedom of choice. I showed Gina my Polaroids and sat on the single chair in the living room. I rarely sat on the couch because Robert expected his legs and feet to be caressed, and I didn't want to touch him in that way. I sat there preoccupied, reliving my experience and wondering whether I'd meet Joe again. I jumped when my reverie was rudely interrupted by Robert.

'Natasha, you seem different since you got back,' he said staring at me from the couch.

I frowned, thinking, *I've only been back a few hours.*

'Gina, why don't you sit with Natasha,' he said curtly.

Gina responded and sat on the arm of my chair. It was like he knew what I was thinking, because he sounded irritated and wanted to distract me from my train of thought by putting Gina at my side. I wondered what difference he saw, as the only thing

I could think of was the boost of confidence I had gained. This seemed to make Robert unsettled, because he liked to control people, but he couldn't control my thoughts, and this gave me a sense of inner empowerment.

'Robert, may I get ready for bed?' I asked, feeling uncomfortable with Gina sitting close and putting her arm around my shoulders.

'Gina, you go up too and run a bath for you both,' he said with an evil glint in his eyes.

The energy in the room became intense, which made me jump up quickly to leave; Gina followed behind me like a lapdog. I missed the country house already, and the freedom I'd had to do as I pleased in the early morning and evening.

'Let's share this bath water, Natasha,' Gina said, removing her clothes and stepping into the bath.

I hesitated, gazing at her; she was always trying her best to lure me towards her.

Gina smiled and looked provocative, while gently circling the water with her hands, 'Get in, Tasha, before it gets cold.'

I felt strange getting into the bath with another person; the last time I shared a bath was with my siblings when we were young. But, as usual, I did what was asked and rationalised that this was normal because we were both girls.

Afterwards, I followed Gina to the kitchen to sort through the vitamins we had to take. Gina made a pile of different tablets for each person, and it was only now that I became curious and asked what each one was for. Gina told me they were Kalms (although I didn't realise at the time that these are a form of sedative), water-retention tablets to keep us slim, and multivitamins, vitamin C and cod liver oil that were beneficial for our health.

***

I noticed that, during the week, it was just Cassandra and me who stayed at the house; I missed the others and looked forward to their arrival at the weekends. I often wondered what they thought about the close relationship between Gina and I, and wished I could kick her away from my ankles, so I could just hang out with girls my age. Many times, I felt awkward when I asked to get ready for bed first. I hoped I could go up on my own or with the other girls, only I was soon disappointed when Robert sent Gina up with me. And, although I already knew the answer to my question about which bedroom I was sleeping in, I always asked in the hope of Robert reprieving me by saying I was back with the girls again. I was stuck in a shameful prison that I felt I couldn't get out of, and the only chance I had of being set free was the fact I was now a professional model and could get away when I worked.

Reflection

The last phase of grooming is the offender maintaining control to avoid detection, so they can carry on with the abusive behaviour. They've invested a lot of time and money, and won't let go of their victims easily. Robert manipulated the environment I lived in, and I felt suffocated that I no longer had the freedom to do what I wanted. My abusers kept me close, so I barely spent time with my parents. The more cut off I was, the more he gained power over me, because I wasn't with my family long enough to process and question anything outwardly. This meant I wouldn't be influenced by support networks outside the groomers' sphere of influence (the modelling agency in this case), which is common in grooming.

It was like the girls and I were in a cult, and being groomed into obedience; we followed the leader because we were showered with compliments, promises of a bright future, and nights out when we were plied with food and drink. This is similar to the 'party lifestyle' model where minors are groomed in a group, only they're unaware that the perpetrator wants repayment at some point, which is often sexual.

I was entangled in a relationship with my groomers that prevented me from confronting their sexual comments and advances. I knew it wasn't right that the relationship had become sexualised, but I was ashamed and too embarrassed to tell anyone. This situation is extremely hard to get out of when autonomy has been stripped away. When living in a paedophile's world, you're in a haze of confusion. If you find yourself experiencing this, then note that it's wrong for people to take away your identity. If I had my time again, I'd speak to someone and save myself from suffering any more abuse.

8

SPECIAL FAVOURITES

By December 1993, the girls and I were well established as a group, and we enjoyed each other's company. Even though it was freedom from our families, it was very much controlled by Robert. Two new girls under 16 became regulars, and they merged into our group, which was getting older now – we were between 16 and 18. During this time, Robert became more daring with his behaviour, by teasing and touching the girls in a playful way, which none protested to. However, I sat back and watched his antics, trying to figure out my conflicted feelings as to whether I loved or hated him.

It was a full house one Saturday night, and I sat on the steps that divided the living room and dining room; my usual seat had been taken by one of the new girls. There was space on the couch, but I avoided it because Robert lay on it, with Gina and Cassandra by his feet. Cassandra always showed him loving affection, and I wondered what she saw in him. Robert flicked from channel to channel, and I noted he never asked anyone if there was something they wanted to watch.

To our surprise and dismay, Robert stopped at a porn channel. I felt the awkwardness in myself and the other girls in the room. I briefly looked at the screen, on which there were naked men and women groaning, while having wild group sex. I could see he was amused, yet I didn't want to give him the satisfaction of looking completely away, even though I was embarrassed. Robert seemed to like the discomfort in the room; however, he didn't keep it on for long, but it was long enough for us to have a lasting image in our heads. He made out he had accidentally come across the channel and chuckled.

Following this, I asked to go to bed. 'Where am I sleeping?' I said, still hoping to be reunited with the girls.

'The usual place,' he replied smugly.

I believe he knew I longed to be out of his room, but kept me in it like it was some sort of punishment for asking.

'And Cassandra will be in the room tonight,' Robert added, smiling devilishly, leaving me unsure how to read his face.

I walked to his bedroom, curious about the change in the sleeping arrangements. I wondered who Gina would be sharing with, and couldn't see why Cassandra would want to share a bed with Robert.

I drifted off to sleep, but stirred as Cassandra got into his bed. I roused to the faint sound of Robert whistling merrily in the bathroom. The more I tried to sleep, the more alert I became. I pretended to be slumbering, because I didn't want to engage in conversation with them; however, I wished I had that night.

They were talking, and I was sure they were trying to wake me. I squeezed my eyes shut and tried to sleep, but I was too irritated by them. I stared at the wall, now that my eyes were accustomed to the dark room; the only light was the light seeping through the curtains. Their chatter faded, which was a relief, until I heard the squelching sound of cream, which made me freeze and my eyes glared at the wall. I knew the sound of what was to come next. Cassandra moaned as he entered her and began to thrust hard, shaking the bed. I didn't know what to do, it drove me insane with every thrust he made. I was hot and angry under the duvet, and the voice in my head was screaming at me to get up, but my body was like a lead weight.

Robert said, 'Look, Cassandra, Tasha is over there,' and he began breathing deeply as he thrusted harder to make Cassandra moan louder.

I wanted to shout out, 'My name is Claire,' but my voice wouldn't rise from my throat.

'What a turn on, Cassandra,' Robert said pounding faster like she was a piece of meat. 'We're fucking, and she is over there; we could wake her!' he added, panting and clearly turned on that I was so close.

I willed him to stop, but stayed still, in a state of shock. From that moment on, I felt claustrophobic sharing a room, and any noise drove me crazy; I hated him with a vengeance that night.

***

The next morning, I was determined not to give Robert any satisfaction and acted as though I hadn't been awake during his antics. I had been sure he had slept with some of the previous group of girls, and now Cassandra in our group; this confirmed that my hunch that Cassandra had been sleeping with him for some time was right. It was like he singled everyone out to make them feel special; however, I knew there was no way I'd sleep with him.

From this experience, pressure began to build in my mind with all my unspoken feelings and thoughts. And, even though I tried to repress them, they turned into headaches that were willing me to find my voice. I seemed stuck, and had no one to share my inner world with or express what was going on externally in the evil, perverted world I was living in.

***

During the Christmas holidays of 1993, I stayed home with my family; I had missed the normality of family life. Even though it felt like a sanctuary, I couldn't switch off from Robert and Gina. I kept having waves of wondering what people would think if I was frank about what I was experiencing at the models' house. The loss of my voice scared me, but I knew somehow that, if I were to find it, I'd be bombarded with questions from adults who would have alarm bells ringing. Thoughts crossed my mind of ways I could eventually escape, but I felt trapped, and unable to control my body and mind. The only thing that kept me going was the thought of travelling to Asia.

***

At the beginning of January 1994, I happily watched Gina organise my contracts and draw up a spreadsheet to make it clear where I'd be throughout the year: from 26th January I'd be in Tokyo for two months, it would be Korea in June, then I'd fly to Osaka in August for two months. It was becoming an exciting and daunting reality, looking at the amount of time I'd be away.

After signing the contracts, Gina received a call from another Manchester agency called Image One Models. Robert and Gina weren't happy about this. Yuki had told them I was going to Tokyo, and they phoned to say they had a model of the same age, called Sarah, who was going too. They suggested that we travel together, considering it was our first trip away. Gina told me that she and Robert thought it best we didn't, because it was a rival, where Elaine, the old booker, was working.

I couldn't see the problem and liked the idea of making new friends, and travelling wouldn't feel so daunting if I had a companion. Again, I didn't voice my thoughts.

The following week, my mind ticked over again when I felt a stab of envy as Sarah from Image One Models appeared on a local TV programme with her manager, talking about her opportunity to go to Japan. I wondered why Gina hadn't been in touch with the local news, so the modelling agency could receive some good publicity too.

***

My portfolio became fully professional when Mike sent the bridal brochure to the modelling agency, and I was able to add my first tear sheet into it.

'Look what's arrived, Tasha,' Gina exclaimed, holding a large envelope.

My eyes widened as I walked over to take it from her. 'Let me open it,' I said with a grin.

'No, I will,' she said, smiling, and covered the envelope, so I couldn't see. Gina seemed to be teasing me, but I didn't find it amusing. She opened it, still covering it from my sight.

I scowled, and Gina looked at me playfully. I stood there wondering why she did this, then Robert emerged from his office to take a look. Their control by not letting me see filled me with frustration and a force that wanted to lash out at them, but I had to stay contained like the good, compliant child I was.

'These pictures are really good,' Robert said as he flicked through the pages.

I gritted my teeth through a smile as I was standing behind them. When I finally got to look, I reminisced about the shoot and wondered what Joe might be doing; I smiled wickedly, knowing they didn't know what I was thinking. I couldn't wait to get home and show my parents.

When I did, Mum rushed to the local shop and bought all the brochures off the shelf to give to family and friends. I was proud that one of my goals at the beginning of my journey had been achieved. Now, I waited to reach another: to fly across the world and begin the interesting life of a model through pictures.

***

When my passport arrived, I had to go to the Japanese Embassy in London to apply for my visa. My parents couldn't accompany me because of work; however, Robert told me it'd be good for me to travel alone.

'Tash, you can go by coach, as it's cheaper. You don't have to ask your parents for money, as I'll pay, and I'll give you a mobile phone, so we can get hold of you and make sure you're safe.' He conveyed this like it was already planned. Robert handed me the phone and extra money to spend while I was in the capital for the day.

'Ring me if you get into trouble or need anything, and we'll see you later this evening. I'll pick you up from the coach station,' he added seeing me to the door.

I fell into the busy streets of Manchester city centre and walked the short distance to the coach station, hoping I had all the visa paperwork. This was the first time I felt fully grown up, as I was doing something without the help of someone by my side.

***

London was an adventure; everything was new and I was swept away with the fast pace of life. I had a few hiccups, as I travelled by Tube in the wrong direction, and I had to leave the Japanese Embassy to take copies of documents and get passport pictures. I hadn't a clue what I was doing or where I was going to find any places to help me complete my application. It was a case of learning from the experience, so I got it right the next time. I explored the capital for a while; it seemed so big and scary compared to Manchester. Southern hustle and bustle was on a different level from what I was used to in my home town; I felt quite small in the big city. I found a bench in Green Park to eat my lunch and pulled the phone from my bag. I had missed calls from the office and so I called back immediately.

'Hi Natasha, how has your day been so far?' Robert said cheerfully.

'Good; the embassy told me I should receive my stamped passport in ten days,' I replied.

'That's great, what time will you be back?' Robert asked eagerly.

'Around 8pm, I think,' I stated, and looked in my bag for my ticket.

'Great, ring me if there are any delays. See you later, Tasha.' The phone rang off, and I sat eating happily and watching the world go by.

***

Later that night, after a successful rest of day, I was exhausted when the coach pulled into the station and surprised to see Robert alone, waiting for me at the pick-up point.

'Hi Tasha,' he said smiling, holding a glass of brandy and Coke.

'Hello,' I replied, noticing the frothy substance on the rim of the glass.

'Here, this is for you. I thought you might need it after being in London,' he added, handing me the glass.

I took a sip and was glad it didn't taste as strong as he usually made it.

'Let's sit here while you finish your drink, and you can tell me all about London.'

He seemed over-interested in what I had to say, which made me feel strange as I sat with him. I wondered why we didn't go straight to the house, rather than sitting there and him watching me drink every last drop. He stood, taking the empty glass, and we walked briskly towards the modelling agency. The evening was coming alive, with people heading into bars and restaurants. He opened the front door to the building as people scurried past.

'You go up, Tasha; Gina is there, but I'm going out for a while,' he said letting me in.

The building was dark, and it looked ghostly as I walked to the lift. I opened the reception door, feeling tired, and longing to have a shower and go to bed, but Robert and Gina had other plans. I found Gina waiting in her underwear with brandies and cigarettes; she passed me a drink and asked about my day. Taking the drink from her, I noticed the frothy head again.

Gina distracted my observation by saying, 'Natasha, have a look in this bag, take something you like and put it on.'

I looked towards an open bag in the middle of the room. My mind backtracked as I pulled out lace and satin underwear.

It was the same black bag I had briefly caught a glimpse of in Robert's office, when he pushed it under the draped curtain.

I was struggling to determine how I felt as I looked at the different sets of underwear, stockings, suspenders, heeled shoes and bottles of Chanel No. 5 that were half empty. The whole experience was overwhelming me, and I certainly wasn't in the mood for what lay ahead; I was grumpy and hadn't eaten since lunch.

'Drink up, Tasha, so we can spend some time together before Robert gets back,' Gina said as she leant on the side cabinet looking suggestive, while I sat on the reception chair and sipped the brandy, which made me heave from the strong, sweet smell.

I gulped down the liquid and my stomach churned. I lit a cigarette to help numb the taste of brandy and the overpowering scent of Chanel No. 5.

'Drink some more, Tash,' Gina pushed.

I wanted to carry on smoking for as long as I could, because I didn't want to have sex with her. I had experienced enough and didn't want to continue with a woman who now stood before me looking like a high-class prostitute. I defiantly blew out the cigarette smoke towards her and took another sip of brandy. The smell and taste hit my stomach, and I became nauseated. Gina knocked back her drink and waited patiently. I looked into her eyes and took another drag of my cigarette, feeling a different vibe from her compared to other times; she was rushing me, which I didn't like.

'Down it, Natasha, you haven't much left,' Gina commanded, seeming eager to get her perverted hands on me.

But I was basking in the control of forcing her to wait, so I had less time with her in the back room. She watched my every move, and there was a small part of me that felt sorry for her while I took my time. I took the last gulp and was nearly sick when it entered my throat; this last bit of brandy seemed to take effect and went straight to my head, making me feel dizzy.

Gina led me into the dark catwalk room, and I was hesitant; the only light came from the back room, where they were on full beam. I squinted at the brightness, and I thought new bulbs must have been put in. I didn't like it because I felt exposed and more on show under the lights. The room was laid out differently from before. This time, the blankets and pillows were facing the filing cabinet. My head spun as I undressed, and through my dizziness I wondered why Gina wanted me in underwear when she was going to take them off. Gina released her bra and I lay on my tummy, comforted by the soft pillow on my cheek, I could have blissfully fallen asleep if Gina hadn't tried to arouse me.

'Tasha, lie on your back,' she said.

I felt muddled because she always started with a back massage. This time she was rushing to do other things, and I began to feel waves of sickness as she hastily played with and caressed my body, while arousing herself at the same time. I didn't have the strength to do anything, apart from concentrating on not throwing up. Gina had stepped up a gear in her seduction, which made me think she was a pro at this sort of stuff. Gina took my hand to make me take part, and I responded in some way, feeling dazed and confused. I gulped, bile rose in my throat as she put on a performance so I could see her body in all its glory, which made me close my eyes in disgust.

Gina was getting nowhere and whatever she was saying sounded muffled in my mind. 'Are you OK, Tash? Let's just lie here.' She sat holding me up against her body, and caressed my chest and nipples, but couldn't reach my genitals when she tried. The more she stroked the more my head started to spin and the more my stomach churned; I knew then that I wasn't going to make it to the toilet. I tried to focus on the filing cabinet, but whatever didn't agree with me that day made my upper body rise and I threw up everywhere. I heaved again, extracting the last bit of brandy, and lay there exhausted. Moments passed in a haze of nothingness, until Gina's voice entered my consciousness.

'Do you think you'll be sick again?' she asked.

'No, I just need some water,' I replied. I stared at the ceiling trying to focus.

Gina left the room, and I sat up facing the filing cabinet surrounded by sick.

Gina returned fully clothed, with water and towels to clean up the mess. I took a sip, but felt like I was going to vomit again. I slowly dressed and glanced in the mirror; I looked terrible.

We went back out to reception, and not many words were exchanged as we waited there for Robert's return. I nervously looked towards the door when I heard the lift ascend. Robert stepped from the lift, and I watched through the glass window as his facial expression changed from surprise to a frown. He waltzed into reception, with his eyes ablaze with anger.

'Why are you both in here?' he shouted.

Before I could muster some words from my weakened state, Gina answered, 'Natasha hadn't eaten this afternoon and the brandy made her sick from having an empty stomach.'

Robert's eyes looked menacing as he stared at me and shouted, 'Why didn't you tell me you hadn't eaten, you silly girl?'

I gulped, feeling frightened; I hadn't been spoken to in this way before.

Robert started ranting and stormed into his office, slamming the door behind him. I heard a cabinet door close and wondered what he was doing. My head began to throb and I wanted to go home, but not to the models' house, just home to be with my parents.

Robert charged from his office, making me jump, shouting, 'After all that I do for you both: I go out of my way to arrange nights out, you go clothes shopping, to aerobics and eat out!'

His list of rants faded into the background of my mind as I concentrated on not vomiting again. He stomped into the back room and I wondered what his problem was to be flying into such a rage. I was sick, but that was no cause to go on and start throwing things in my face.

'You both get everything you want, and I ask for nothing in return,' he added returning to reception and lighting a cigarette. He glared at me before entering his office.

What an idiot, I thought, *I've never asked for any of it, especially creating a night so Gina could use my body to gratify herself.* My thoughts drifted to Tokyo; this was a safe haven in my head that no one could get to. The 26th January couldn't come quick enough, when I'd be flying 6,000 miles away from them.

Reflection

A paedophile's aim, once they're the dominant figure, is to use everything in their power to make sure their victims remain compliant to their sordid behaviour. They use this influence to manipulate and intimidate their prey further with aggression, which makes their victims too paralysed to do anything. During the beginning stages of grooming, Robert lured us to his home and offered us a sense of security, though we ended up as robots brainwashed into obedience.

Being in a group, we felt safe; however, some sex offenders use this as a cunning plan, so that their prey will regard any advances towards them as day-to-day occurrences. As an established group, Robert knew we wouldn't protest about anything he did; we had built mutual trust and friendships, because we had spent a lot of time together and had become like a sisterhood. This was part of Robert's grooming structure, so he felt confident that none of the models he had befriended and controlled in the previous and present groups would have the courage to speak up.

If you experience this kind of group setting, confide in each other no matter how terrified you are of the perpetrator(s); this isn't a place anyone should find themselves in. You can leave and get support if you find the bravery to reach out to the right people. However, this is easier said than done when one is living in a nightmare.

On reflection, I understand my younger self was a frightened teenager faced with an unpredictable predator who could become aggressive at any time. It's hard to leave the clutches of a sex offender, but even harder to stay in the abusive relationship that destroys your soul further the longer the abuse goes on.

9
WORLDS APART

On 25th January 1994, I prepared for my departure. I looked at the two large suitcases lying in my parents' dining room, and wondered if I had everything. Robert and Gina had offered to take me to the airport when I arrived at the modelling agency to pick up copies of my contract; however, I declined, telling them my uncle and parents were taking me.

'Natasha, we have a meal tonight with some important clients, why don't you come along with us, and we can say goodbye properly, since we won't be there to see you off at the airport?' Robert asked, studying me intently. 'And we'll drop you off later,' he added.

I hesitated. 'I… I think my parents are doing a meal for me tonight.'

Robert frowned, making me feel bad. 'We won't be staying out long, so you won't be home too late,' he confirmed.

I watched as his face softened. Robert had a way with words that made me submit and feel guilty for choosing to be with my family. I found myself returning home, and telling my parents I'd be spending the evening with Gina and Robert. They seemed disappointed, and my heart felt torn; I hated upsetting people.

***

On my way to the restaurant, I gazed from the bus window, watching my neighbourhood pass by, and I felt lonely, yet I was glad to have some time to myself. I loved my parents, and even though Robert and Gina were overbearing at times, I had a fondness for them.

***

During the meal, I sat back and looked around the table. *What am I doing?* I thought. The overwhelming guilt washed over me like I was being drowned by a wave, and all I could think about was being home with my family. I began to feel annoyed by my choice to sit with Robert, Gina and two people I didn't care to know. I swallowed deeply to stop myself from crying when one of the clients asked questions about my modelling career and how I felt about going to Japan. My inner voice screamed, *Why am I here? I need to go home.* They became background noise as I grappled with my internal world, longing for the dinner to be over.

***

Once the meal had finished, we left the restaurant. It was dark walking to car. Robert said, 'Gina, you get in the back with Tasha.'

I glared at Robert, wondering what his intent was.

We all got in the car, and – as Robert sped away – Gina began forcing herself onto me. The more she did, the more I shut down. I knew she enjoyed what she was doing, and was doing it for Robert's benefit too. They liked these sex-act performances; it seemed to help with their relationship. Gina tried harder to please me, yet my stubborn nature didn't respond in the way she wanted me to. The guilt and frustration had built up since I had been sitting facing two people I didn't know while picturing my parents at home round the dining table without me. I felt a deep pain in my heart as I saw her determined face. She smiled, and I looked away to find Robert adjusting his rear-view mirror; the evil glint in his eye and his smirk made me angry. He looked to be satisfying his perversion as Gina rubbed over my clothes, trying to arouse me and find her way into my knickers, instead she was physically hurting me – the gentle Gina was gone.

I stared from the car window, saw the houses in my neighbourhood and was relieved, only for my heart to be ripped apart as they disappeared out of sight when Robert carried on driving. I willed him to stop and for Gina to realise I wasn't interested in her advances. It seemed he was driving in circles on purpose, and this notion and Gina's persistence made me even more obstinate. The yearning to get home and into my own bed was too strong, and – no matter how much Gina tried to please Robert's and her own perverted ways – I wouldn't respond. Gina eventually released her claws from me when Robert nodded through the rear-view mirror. Even though I was set free, I felt a pain in my chest for not being where I belonged the night before I left my hometown.

Finally, Robert stopped the car outside my parents' house.

'Goodbye, Tasha, I'll miss you,' Gina said as she stepped from the car to let me out.

Robert squeezed my arm as I stretched my legs from the backseat.

'I'll call when you arrive in Japan,' Gina stated, and opened her arms to hug me.

Even though I felt sad and angry, I hugged her back.

'Goodbye Tash,' Robert added.

'Goodbye,' I replied

Gina got back in the car and Robert accelerated away.

As I watched the car drive from my street, I'd never felt so much grief and relief at being home.

I entered a dark house, which brought tears to my eyes. I switched on the light, and saw a few glasses and cups scattered around, and the remains of a meal in the kitchen that I should have had with my family. Silent tears trickled down my face; I felt guilty and so alone walking up the stairs to my room. I didn't want to burst into tears just in case I was unable to control the deep feelings that were surfacing; somehow, I knew I wouldn't be able to stop once the flood gates opened.

***

The following morning, I gathered last minute things, then watched Dad cook breakfast.

'How was last night, Claire?' he asked, frying the eggs.

'It was nice, with good food,' was all I could muster, and I was barely able to look my father in the eyes for fear he would see my distress, which he might question. I wanted to say sorry for not being around, but chose to change the subject quickly before I broke down in tears.

***

I had mixed emotions watching my hometown fade away as we made our way to the airport. I was relieved to be going, but sad to be leaving my family behind. I'd become very distant from them since being with the modelling agency, and now I yearned to feel close to them again.

Thirty minutes later, I checked in at the Virgin desk, feeling nervous. 'Would you like some assistance through transit as you're young and travelling alone?' the lady behind the counter asked and she studied my face for an answer.

'Yes,' I said awkwardly, as I wasn't sure if I needed help. It seemed as if I was being treated like a child, yet being given the choice to be an adult and to do things by myself.

A little later, at passport control, I hugged my uncle goodbye, then turned to my father, who took me into a protective embrace.

'Look after yourself, Claire,' he said, holding me tight.

Tears stung my eyes. How soothing it was to hear my real name and feel genuine protection. I faced my mum, and she began to cry, which made me gulp back my own tears. I didn't want to cry in public – I wanted to stay strong – but the warm tears rolled down my cheeks as she hugged me closer.

If only my tears were for leaving and not because she had no clue what had been happening to me. Questions raced through my mind; how could I tell Mum my agents had me totally confused about everything: who I was, my sexuality and my loss of innocence? Gina and Robert had violated me, and I felt powerless to break free. Mum released me; I hated seeing her upset.

I hurried through passport control and turned one last time to wave goodbye, before disappearing into the departure gate with tears rolling down my face, and hearing Mum's faint sobs in the distance.

I walked across to the windows of the departure gate, and I studied the plane as I waited to board. It was my first time to fly on a Boeing 747. I pulled out the camera Dad had given me and took a picture of the Maiden of Honour printed on the side of the plane, who was flying with ease. I was ready to fly away, even though I felt broken.

***

Twelve hours later, I landed at Narita airport. Walking into unknown territory, I was a little intimidated by Immigration asking questions before stamping my passport. When I reached the arrivals lobby, there was a short Japanese man holding a name card with 'Natasha' written on it. I felt a stab of pain at not seeing 'Claire', but quickly accepted the fact that, in the modelling world, I'd be someone else.

'Hi,' I said brightly, walking towards him.

'Hello, I'm Mr Watanabe. I'll be your driver,' he replied, then whipped a suitcase from my hand and started to walk briskly through the crowds.

After we had reached his car and set off, I attempted at making conversation whilst being chauffeured into the city.

'No speak English, please rest,' he said glancing in his rear-view mirror.

I tried to sleep, but the landscape awakened my curiosity as it changed from mountains, temples, traditional Japanese houses and industrial estates. I hadn't a clue what to expect and was amazed, soaking up the skyline as we headed into the buzzing city of Tokyo, with its skyscrapers standing side by side.

***

We arrived at the apartment before noon. Mr Watanabe removed his shoes and I followed suit. I watched him quickly drag my huge suitcase down the hall, and thought what a funny little man he was with his swiftness. I glanced round the apartment; it had a nice ambience. I followed Mr Watanabe as he dragged my second suitcase to my room. He knocked on the sliding door that separated the two bedrooms, and waited for signs of any life that lay behind it. We stared at the door, then at each other; I shrugged my shoulders as he opened the sliding door to find my roommate getting out of bed and scrambling over her mess. I smirked, looking at the chaos in her room and trying to spot the blue carpet.

Mr Watanabe turned and said in broken English, 'This is your roommate; the modelling agency will call soon. Rest.' He bowed and left as swiftly as he had arrived.

'Hi, I'm Tina,' my roommate said, stepping over clothes and shoes.

I replied, 'I'm Natasha; it's nice to meet you,' and shook her hand.

'What part of England are you from, Natasha?' she added, trying to tidy some of the clutter.

'I'm from Manchester,' I confirmed. I smiled and was happy to be sharing with someone who spoke English.

'I'm sorry I can't chat for long; I have to be at the Satu Models in an hour. I was out last night and stayed out longer than I should have,' Tina explained, smiling wickedly. 'It's so much fun here,' she continued and winked. 'OK, I need to get ready for castings now.' Tina left me standing in a bare room that was ready to be filled with my stuff.

I felt so far away from what I knew that I left the apartment with Tina, because I didn't want to be by myself, not knowing what to expect. I was glad the agency wasn't far.

'Do you think you'll be able to find your way back to the apartment, Natasha?' Tina asked as she opened the door to a tall office building. 'This is the place, it's on the fifth floor, and this area is called Roppongi.' Tina's eyes looked mischievous.

'Yes, I think so,' I replied.

'Maybe see you later on castings,' said Tina, and with that she was gone, letting the door close behind her.

I stood there, feeling a little lost, before finding my way back to the apartment.

***

I felt like a caged animal waiting for Satu Models to phone. I wanted to go out, but was afraid of going too far, of not being able to find my way back and of missing the call. Later that afternoon, a booker called Kasumi phoned to tell me that Mr Watanabe would pick me up at 10am, and they would let my mother modelling agency know I had arrived safely.

I waited patiently for Tina's return, but she wasn't in long and told me she was going out with friends. I didn't know what to do with myself; I lay in bed, wide awake, until I decided to get up, look out of the window and smoke a cigarette. I faced the brightly lit advertising boards, and buildings of all shapes and sizes. I couldn't wait to go out and start exploring.

***

At sunrise, I looked through my clothes. I had brought so much, yet I couldn't find anything to wear, after admiring Tina's fashion sense. I switched the TV on and flicked through the channels while I waited for Mr Watanabe. I sat mesmerised by how different the Japanese were. When the doorbell rang, I jumped up, eager to leave.

'*Ohayōgozaimasu*, Natasha-san; this means good morning,' Mr Watanabe said, standing in the doorway.

'Good morning,' I replied, happy to see his friendly face, but not attempting to repeat what he said.

We drove the short distance to the agency; the building seemed familiar, having seen it the day before. We got out of the car, walked inside, found the lifts and took one to the fifth floor. I was a little nervous as the lift doors opened to reveal a dusky-pink office.

A polite Japanese receptionist greeted us with a graceful bow. 'Hello, you must be Natasha; it's nice to meet you,' she said in perfect English.

'Hi,' I replied and followed Mr Watanabe, feeling anxious at seeing models sitting on the couch chatting; they smiled as I tried to walk confidently past. Entering the booking room, I instantly felt welcomed by everyone saying, 'Welcome to Tokyo.' I beamed at all the grinning faces before me.

'Natasha-san,' Chiyo said, approaching me, 'I'm pleased that you're finally here,' and gave me a hug. I liked Chiyo from our meeting in Manchester.

'This is Kasumi; you spoke on the phone with her yesterday. These are Eriko and Etsuko; they're bookers here at Satu Models.'

They bowed, saying, '*Konnichiwa.*'

'Hi,' I replied, immediately feeling safe. I soaked up the office atmosphere; it was lively for first thing in the morning. The round table dominated the centre of the room, and each of the bookers got back to work. Etsuko spun the round shelf attached to the middle of table, and pulled out some files, with paperwork falling out with them. It was organised chaos; phones were ringing and red lights flashed, waiting for someone to pick them up. This office was so unlike my mother modelling agency, which was always spotless and the phones rarely rang.

I ruminated about this for a while, before Kasumi asked me to go with her to sign papers and so she could take my measurements. I liked her, she was bubbly and looked cute as she peered over her glasses to talk to me.

Her eyes cheekily lit up when she laughed, saying, 'My husband is English. I'd like to go to England again one day with my daughter.'

I nodded and spoke a little about my family. She took out her measuring tape and started to measure every part of my body; by now the thoroughness of the Japanese didn't faze me.

'Do you have any hobbies?' Kasumi asked.

I frowned.

'Such as swimming, dancing, skating or ballet?' she added.

'I like swimming and skating, and I go to dance aerobics classes,' I confirmed, though I wasn't sure why this was relevant.

'How long have you been modelling for?' Kasumi asked as she looked over her glasses again.

'I've been with my modelling agency for three years,' I told her.

'Ah, three years, that's a long time! Are you OK doing underwear, nude and fur?' She asked and paused before ticking the boxes on her form.

'I'll do underwear and fur,' I replied.

Kasumi pulled the paperwork together. I didn't recall this much attention to detail with Northern Teen Models and I wondered why this was.

'Oh, I nearly forgot,' she stated, 'Will you sign this? It's a curfew.'

I looked at her, puzzled.

'Because you're under 18, you can't stay out after midnight,' she explained and placed the paper on the table.

I smirked as I signed it. *How funny,* I thought, *I've just travelled halfway across the world without my parents and now I'm being asked to sign a curfew with my Japanese agent.*

***

Once we had finished, I went to reception, where I sat quietly – waiting to go on castings – and scanned the models' cards before me. The girls were beautiful, and I began to doubt myself in comparison to them. My thoughts were interrupted.

'Hey, I'm Maddy; pleased to meet you,' said a girl who had come into reception; her strong American accent threw me for a moment.

'Hi, I'm Natasha,' I replied.

'Oh, you're from England,' she stated and sat down next to me.

'Yes, from Manchester,' I confirmed, but then I stayed silent, too shy to carry on the conversation.

The agency began to fill with models, who made themselves comfy in reception.

Another new arrival said, 'Hi, I'm Carolyn; it's lovely to meet you.' Her Australian accent sounded friendly.

She put out her hand, and I noted how firm her handshake was because she nearly crushed my hand. It was surreal hearing conversations with different accents from around the world.

A tall, broad Japanese man walked towards me, extended his hand and said, 'Hello Natasha-san; I'm Haruma, one of the managers.'

'Hello, it's nice to meet you,' I said, instantly taken by his warm presence and gentle handshake.

He called out from his sheet the names of the girls who would be with him for the day, and I was happy to be one of them.

***

A short while later, seven models were loaded into a car to begin a day of castings. I smiled, taking a seat near the window. I had waited a year for this to happen and now my goal had been achieved. And I was on another path with no one controlling my every move.

***

As the day progressed, I got to know the models and which of them had been to Japan before. I was one of the youngest, and I found myself shadowing the older models. Haruma managed and promoted us on castings, because we didn't speak Japanese; in turn, we would sit or stand as he spoke about us to the clients.

'Haruma, what do *"kawai"* and *"kireina"* mean?' I asked curiously; these words were used frequently throughout the day when the clients looked at our portfolios.

'They were saying you're either cute or beautiful,' he said smiling.

Haruma and I started to bond as he asked questions about my life. He made me feel safe, and I knew I'd be looked after for the next two months.

As we drove through Tokyo, I was wowed by the big city, which was a mass of tall buildings and people dashing from place to place. I watched the sun begin to set, and the city came alive with brightly lit colours. Cars that looked brand new sparkled on the roads. People hailed cabs, and the cabs' doors automatically opened for them to slip inside. For a fast-moving, busy city, I noticed how clean and tidy it was compared to London.

At one of the castings, on the 29th floor of a skyscraper, I went to the toilet, looked down at the technology and wondered what the different buttons were for. I sat down and felt the warm seat kiss my thighs, but the sound of birds chirping puzzled me. I was too apprehensive to touch any of the buttons, and chuckled to myself, imagining a little Japanese person popping up to wash my bum.

The working day ended at around 8pm, after which I phoned home, though I had forgotten about Robert and Gina, until my parents mentioned they had called to let my parents know I had arrived safely.

***

I settled in quickly, and was soon into the Japanese lifestyle of work, eat and sleep. I admired their work ethic of commitment and pride, which gave me a sense of purpose and dedication to my job while I represented their modelling agency.

I noticed I was quieter than the other girls; Haruma would ask if I was OK from time to time. Sometimes, I drifted into my internal world and thought of home. Everything I was experiencing was so unlike Northern Teen Models.

***

After the first week of castings, I was booked for my first job for a magazine. I had been anxious because my contract stated that if I wasn't booked for any work within two weeks, I'd be sent home, which was something I didn't want to happen.

On the morning of my assignment, I had to meet the clients

near Roppongi Subway Station. My sense of direction was terrible, and I took a wrong turning from my apartment, even though I had a map in my hand.

I could hear Chiyo's voice ringing in my ears, saying, 'Don't be late; Japanese people are very punctual and may hold it against you if you are.' She was a tough boss, I thought, and I didn't want to get on the wrong side of her.

Eventually, I got to where I needed to be and made it on time. The location bus pulled up outside Almonds Coffee Shop, where I was welcomed cheerfully by the team, who said, 'Ohayōgozaimasu,' as I boarded.

Today I was shooting with other models, and the clients had booked an interpreter to communicate with us so we knew what to do. Anything we needed was given at a drop of a hat. The make-up artist sent me into heaven by massaging my shoulders and giving me a mini facial. The stylist, Yumi, helped us dress, and I mean literally; I felt special, but like a toddler, as she helped to put my socks on, and held my arm just in case I fell while slipping my foot into a shoe. She put heat pads on my back to keep me warm while shooting outside. I had never experienced anything like it. They couldn't do enough for us, and we certainly received the very-important-person (VIP) treatment. I thought I could get very used to this.

After the shoot, the clients took the team for a late lunch, where I had my first bento-box meal. A selection of meat, rice, vegetables and miso broth sat before me, with chopsticks that I struggled with. I laughed at myself with the clients until Yumi helped me figure them out. I was amused to hear some of the clients slurp their noodles – it wasn't classed as rude, but I thought my mother would be mortified if I returned home slurping my food. The clients dropped me at the subway station, saying, 'O tsukare-samadesu' (meaning thank you for your hard work). I waited happily for Haruma to pick me up to finish the day with more castings. I was certainly living the dream and enjoying the life of a model in Tokyo.

***

Tina was a wild child and fun to be around; she patiently answered all my ongoing questions. She worked most days because she had been many times before, and I found myself using her as role model.

'Natasha, would you like to come out tonight? It's Friday!' Tina's eyes looked mischievous as she asked this.

'I've signed a curfew,' I replied.

'That doesn't matter; the modelling agency won't find out,' said Tina, winking at me persuasively.

'Well, I suppose so; I am on the other side of the world without my parents!' I exclaimed.

I watched Tina apply her make-up; I'd forgotten mine and was waiting for Gina to send some in the post. I had felt self-conscious when they told me to start wearing make-up for castings, because the clients expected everyone to look like their photographs. I looked at my clothes, wondering what to wear. This was a new experience for me; I hadn't considered going clubbing when I packed, and wished I had Gina's wardrobe in front of me.

'Don't forget your composite card, Natasha; you'll need it to get in free to the clubs,' Tina advised.

I was pleased with my first composite card, as I'd never had any printed in Manchester. Gina told us it was fine to use laser-printer copies of our photos to give the clients. I thought it strange that the new group at Northern Teen Models had not had composite cards made.

Once we had finished getting ready and had left the apartment, our first stop in the popular entertainment district was a bar called Gas Panic. Tina knew most of the bartenders, and I stood listening to the loud music while she was in deep conversation with one of the waiters. They gave us free tequila shots; I knocked one back, which made me want to vomit. Girls danced on the bars, and others were told by the bartender to lie back over the bar while he poured vodka into their mouths. One girl choked on the liquid and sprayed it into the air above her eyes. Her friends picked her up and took her to the toilet. I had never witnessed such craziness.

'Come on, Natasha, let's go to another club,' said Tina. She kissed her friends goodbye, and we slipped back out onto the busy streets of Roppongi. I loved the energy; the Japanese certainly knew how to let their hair down after a hectic week. By now, people were buzzing with 'Friday-night fever'.

'That's Java Jive over there; we can get in free with our comp card,' explained Tina. She took my arm because I was losing sight of her through the crowds.

We walked a little further.

'Here's Lexington Queen [Lex]; everyone comes here!' Tina exclaimed as she dragged me down a few steps to the entrance. 'Hi Bob, how are you?' Tina said to the man on the door, kissing him on both cheeks.

'Hi Tina, I'm fine; it's getting busy down there, so be ready for another fun night,' Bob added in his mild American accent.

I couldn't work out his age, but I guessed he could be in his 50s.

'This is Natasha,' Tina continued.

'Hey, it's nice to meet you,' he said in a friendly manner, which I warmed to.

'Hello, it's nice to meet you too,' I replied, and I followed Tina down the stairs.

She told me he had a genuine love of people and loved models using the club. It had become a popular destination for foreign celebrities, rock stars and Japanese *tarento* (meaning talent).

Tina and I showed our composite cards to the man at the till, and he made sure it was us on the cards before giving us free-drink tickets. Tina headed to the bar, and I stopped to look at the picture collages on the walls, dating back to 1980, of all the celebrities and models who had come to Lex.

While Tina was talking, I waited at the bar to be served; I loved the fact she knew a lot of people. I followed her to the back of the club and sat down on the sofas in the VIP area, holding my drink like it was some sort of protection. Tina introduced me to some of her friends, and – from that moment on – I relaxed into the atmosphere, and started to get a taste for partying all night and living life in the fast lane. We received lots of attention in the VIP area, and I could see how easy (and dangerous) it was for girls to go wild, because we didn't have to pay for anything. I felt like a free spirit getting lost in the music and dancing like nothing else mattered.

I was acutely aware of the male models, and was intimidated when they approached to make conversation, which I couldn't hold for more than 15 minutes. They made me nervous with their confidence and extreme good looks, so I kept my distance at times.

***

One Saturday night, Tina and I headed out in the freezing weather to her friend's apartment to hang out and have a few drinks before going on to the clubs. At the apartment, I sat watching them do drugs. I had not seen drugs taken with plastic bottles and knives before; however, this satisfied my curiosity as to why there were burnt knives in the kitchen drawer at our apartment.

'Here, Natasha, would you like to try?' Tina offered.

'No thanks,' I said lighting a cigarette and taking a sip of vodka. This was something I consciously chose not to get into, and I wondered what my parents would think of me being in this situation.

***

It had surprised me that I was getting away with going out most weekends. Early one morning, I was called into the agency. I felt nervous because they sounded concerned.

'Hi Natasha-san, how are you?' Chiyo asked and signalled for me to sit. 'It's OK,' she said with a smile, 'Your booker from Northern Teen Models has been in touch and they're very angry.' She now looked serious.

'Huh,' I said and pouted.

'They're not happy because they've been trying to call you most weekends and during weekday evenings, and you haven't answered the phone,' Chiyo explained.

She seemed to be telling me off, but somehow I realised she was cool about things. Even though I had signed a curfew, it was common knowledge that Asia is extremely safe; it was just some of the foreigners you had to look out for.

'They've asked for you to be moved to a different apartment and for you not to share with Tina, because they said she is a bad influence on you, so we've agreed to this for your last few weeks here,' Chiyo added.

My face dropped.

Chiyo continued, 'If you can pack today, we'll have Mr Watanabe move your stuff to the apartment in Azabu-Jūban.' She smiled. 'You'll have a new roommate called Brooke arriving tomorrow from Canada. Oh, and you've been booked for a catalogue shoot, so well done.' Chiyo stood and patted my arm before returning to her office.

I was annoyed with Robert and Gina for embarrassing me; what would I say to Tina? I knew that changing apartments wouldn't stop me going out, as Azabu-Jūban is only a 20-minute walk from Roppongi. And, no matter what they said at home, the rebel inside me wanted to play and not be told what to do while I was away.

***

Brooke and I were the same age, and instantly clicked. Brooke was a confident 16-year-old, seemed worldlier than me and was ready to hit the nightlife of Tokyo straight away.

When we went out, Brooke and I bumped into Tina at Java Jive. I preferred this club to Lex because it had two floors, and more space to dance and live in the moment, not thinking of the past or future.

'I hear your modelling agency back home thinks I was a bad influence on you,' Tina said, winking.

'Yes, apparently so,' I agreed.

Tina and I giggled at me being out, and hung out for a while. I had never experienced so much fun with a range of people from around the world. When we had used our free-drink tickets, there was always someone close by that wanted to buy us a drink. I compared this to what happened back home. I had fun with the Manchester models, but that was controlled under Robert's supervision. In Tokyo, I had the freedom to roam where I pleased.

***

However, during my stay, I missed home when I wasn't busy with work and castings, and would find myself hiding boxes of chocolates and then comfort eating alone. It wasn't long until the modelling agency commented on my weight gain and measured me. I was mortified when Kasumi asked me to lose weight because I had gained an inch all over.

At lunchtime that day, I told Brooke how worried I was about losing weight. I then found myself returning to the apartment to make myself sick, but every time I put my fingers down my throat nothing came up. After a third attempt, I gave up and screamed, 'What the hell am I doing? This is stupid; I love my food.' I made myself a promise that I wouldn't let myself be that girl who became obsessed trying to please people and lose weight by throwing up.

***

A week before my scheduled departure, I had no work booked, and so Satu Models told me I could go home early. I hadn't made much money, but this didn't bother me because it wasn't the money I was chasing. It was the experience of learning about a new modelling lifestyle and culture that now warmed my heart.

Mr Watanabe drove me to the airport, and I gazed from the window, reminiscing about my trip. I had learnt more in two months here than in three years at Northern Teen Models. As we crossed the Rainbow Bridge, I looked at the skyline, and felt a little embarrassed that I hadn't done much sightseeing or taken many pictures. Although I was excited to return home, I felt a little sad at leaving the people I had grown to respect. However, I was happy because Chiyo had asked me to return once I gained more experience, and I had more tear sheets in my portfolio.

Reflection

After three years of grooming, Robert had gained ultimate power over me by controlling what I did. He had succeeded in keeping me away from my family and friends, and now he was beginning to control my movements while I was away. His tactic shifted more towards aggression, which was to maintain the tight rein he already had. And, even when I was abroad, his anger from afar still unconsciously controlled me. Like some other perpetrators of abuse, Robert saw me as his possession, and he was determined to keep me close and make me his conquest one day. He was a master of deceit, and clever at showing the outside world his charm and attentiveness, while knowing what he was doing in seducing young girls was wrong. He behaved in a way that showed no regard to the emotional and physical damage he was inflicting on his targets.

As young as I was, I reflected on the differences between the agencies; however, I didn't trust my intuition or have the confidence to say Northern Teen Models didn't seem normal when I then had another modelling agency to compare it to. The grooming I had experienced blurred the lines around the abuse, and I was unable to see that Gina forcing herself on me for her sexual gratification and my resisting her advances was a sexual assault. The relationship I had with her and my naivety made it difficult to identify and talk about what was happening.

If you have been or are in this position, then it's wrong for anyone to force themselves on you against your will. Even if you think you may love them, know that it was the sex offender's plan from the very beginning to manipulate an emotional bond between you, before taking away your autonomy over the months or years of grooming, so they could gain control. Please note that, once this has gone, they'll never give it back.

10

BROKEN

Touching down in Manchester, I had butterflies in my stomach. I was like an excited child wanting to get home, tell my parents all about my trip and receive some affirmations. I also had my birthday to look forward to. When I met them in arrivals, I embraced my parents and hugged them for a little while. I had felt awful before I left, and had ruminated for some time about the wrong choice I made to join Robert and Gina for dinner, rather than be with my family.

We left the airport and, as we drove towards my neighbourhood, something within me felt different; it was like things hadn't changed here, but they had changed for me. I looked at my community through a different lens; I was happy to see my roots, but branching out had expanded my outlook and in some ways I felt like an outsider. Since joining the modelling agency, I'd been given a bigger canvas to play with, and the goals and dreams I'd painted onto it were now a reality.

***

I hadn't been home long when Gina rang to check on me. She asked for Natasha, and again I became annoyed with her because I was called Claire at home. My parents weren't about to call their daughter by a different name.

'Hi Natasha, how was your flight?' Gina said brightly.

'It was long and I'm tired; I can't wait to jump into bed.' I was short with my answers because I wanted to get off the phone quickly.

'Do you think you'll be in at the weekend? It'd be great if you could tell the girls in the classes all about your trip,' Gina added.

'Yes, I'll come in, but I have to go now. See you on Saturday,' I confirmed, and then I hung up.

***

A few days later, on my birthday, I reflected on the past year and then looked forward to what my 17th year would bring.

It was hard to imagine that, three years previously, I had walked nervously into the modelling agency with Leanne, when I was now walking in feeling confident and proud.

I knew the girls would benefit from it and find it inspiring when I talked about modelling in Japan. I sat with them, answering their questions and explaining about the life of a model in Tokyo, but avoided talking about the party scene on purpose. Robert and Gina had made it clear that they weren't happy with me for having a taste of the nightlife.

Now that I was a professional model representing the modelling agency, I began sitting with Gina in the classes and interviews. Gina was like a proud parent showing my portfolio to the girls who came to be aspiring models. I liked this attention; their eyes glowed with admiration because they could be in my shoes one day. I sensed some of the parents were just as eager for their daughters to achieve the same goal.

***

The weekends started to get back into the same old routine as before my trip, and a few new girls became regulars at the house, which made it feel overcrowded. I felt unsettled; it was like another group was forming and the old group was moving out. Many times, I was lost in my thoughts and found myself looking into the mirror like I had done before, asking why I was there and wondering who I was in those changing times.

One evening, I lay in bed sleepless, because Robert was reading. I turned over a few times, but I couldn't get comfortable. I longed to be in one of the other bedrooms or at home.

Gina sensed my frustration, saying, 'Robert, I'm going to turn over and go to sleep.' Gina kissed him goodnight.

'Good night, love,' he said, turning a page.

Gina slipped her hand under the duvet and stroked my hand while I drifted off to sleep.

Later, I was startled from my slumber to find Gina and Robert fighting. I focused on their shadows in the darkness, as Robert dragged Gina from the bed by her hair and into the bathroom. I lay there, stunned and frightened, and pretended to be asleep still.

I heard his muffled voice say, 'You don't have to hold her hand in the night, and when I want sex with you, I'll have you; don't ever push me away.'

I wasn't able to hear Gina's response, as they went downstairs and into the living room, which was below their bedroom.

I heard his voice say faintly, 'I'll fuck you here without her around.'

In his rage, he entered Gina hard because she let out a shriek. I put my hands over my ears so I couldn't hear them having sex.

***

The following morning, I looked knowingly at Gina. I noticed some scratches and bruises on her body, but didn't say anything. Robert's face was like thunder, which scared me, because now I'd witnessed an unpredictable violence in him. All I could do was act oblivious to what had happened; I felt like I was coming between them, which wasn't my fault. I never wanted to be tangled in the middle of a perverted love triangle.

***

During the week, I was restless and bored because the office was lifeless. Again, I was curious about this when I compared it to Satu Models, but still I couldn't bring myself to question anything outwardly. This muteness frustrated me, and even more so when Robert approached me while I sat at the reception desk. He knelt on the step facing me and began taunting me. I stared into his eyes, hoping he would pick up the fact that I disliked him at times.

'You don't like me today do you, Tasha?' he said smirking.

'No, I don't,' I replied, frowning. He was so close that I could have quite happily hit him over the head with the phone that was by my hand.

Gina laughed to try to diffuse the tension in the room, while I sat there seething as Robert stood and walked away cockily, chuckling to himself.

On other occasions, Robert would grab me, either at the house or in the office, and force himself onto me. He would tussle me to the ground and lie on top of me, grabbing my arms to make them flat, while I struggled underneath him. He read my grapples like it was something I enjoyed. I'd kick, bite and do anything to get his weight off me. Again, Robert found this amusing, like it was some sort of game, and Gina just watched, doing nothing to help get him off me. I glared at her thinking, *How could she stay with this man for so long, knowing that he slept with others and was now mauling me?* Again, I wondered how I could find a way to leave. I was so scared because all I was able do was repress everything, and more so now because of his violent streak. Staying silent was the safer option, rather than opening Pandora's box to a complete nightmare.

***

By the end of May, I had slipped back into the clutches of Robert and Gina, while my family remained in the background. However, I was looking forward to mid-June and fulfilling my contract to go to Korea for a month. Some of the other models were there already, and I was itching to join them.

'Gina, I was wondering if you've booked my flight ticket for Korea?' I asked needily.

'No, I haven't,' Gina said, looking surprised.

Robert interrupted, 'Korea? We didn't think you wanted to go. You've been sunbathing and you know Asia likes pale skin! And you haven't mentioned wanting to go away again.' Robert's interruption cut the conversation short.

I was speechless and screamed in my mind; I shouldn't have had to mention this, because it was on the spreadsheet Gina made earlier in the year – what a control freak! I was annoyed at myself for letting them control me, when my parents didn't tell me what to do with my life. I wanted to express myself, and tell Gina I'd had enough, was ashamed being around her and didn't want to engage in sexual acts with her any more. But I was so desensitised, through the special relationship she had developed with me and from seeing her as a best friend, that I didn't have the courage to pull away.

***

A few weekends before my trip, Robert decided we should eat at the models' house rather than going out. While Gina cooked, the girls and I were getting tipsy. The alcohol was affecting me differently because, since I'd been back, things felt different within the group, and I felt little pushed out. My instincts told me that one of the girls my age had slept with him, but nothing was discussed between any of us. It seemed our closeness at the beginning had disintegrated somehow; however, I was proud of myself for not sleeping with him.

After supper, Robert took his usual place on the sofa. *He's so cocky*, I thought, as I looked over from where I sat. Beth had her back against the arm of my chair. We were fond of each other because we had started to stay at the house at around the same time, and she was the joker of the group. However, Beth didn't stay at the house frequently because she became loud and boisterous when she got drunk, and Robert didn't like to put up with her unpredictable behaviour. Beth and I were in close conversation, and I could see from the corner of my eye that Robert was observing us. Beth stood up for herself and would answer him back if he provoked her, though she seemed to push him too far this time and Robert put her in her place. Through the noise of the TV and the other girls talking, I could see Robert and Gina chatting; I scowled because I didn't like the way he treated Beth as an outsider.

'Natasha and Beth, go up and get ready for bed,' Robert said sternly. This made a nice change from going up with Gina, and we left the room giggling. I was delighted because I thought I'd be staying in the top bedroom with Beth, but I was soon disappointed when Gina came up.

'Here, girls, take these vitamins,' she said.

I didn't bother asking which ones they were, but placed all the vitamins in my mouth and washed them down with water. Gina had told me this was the best way to take them. I watched Beth take hers one by one, and was sure she was doing this on purpose.

'Do I have to take these?' Beth fired at Gina.

'Yes, they're good for you. Also, you're both sleeping in Robert's room tonight,' she said. She took our glasses and told us to go to his room.

Beth looked mortified; I smiled as if to reassure her that it was OK. I laughed and jumped into the single bed, saying, 'This is my bed; you're there.' I pointed to the double bed.

'I'm not sleeping in his bed,' she said with a strong northern accent. Beth looked dismayed and sat on my bed.

Gina entered the room, 'Goodnight, girls; Tasha, you get in the double bed, and, Beth, you sleep in the single.'

My face dropped as I watched Gina leave the room and turn out the light. I climbed into the double bed, feeling weird taking Gina's spot, and squashed myself against the single bed and pulled the covers over my shoulders, saying over and over in my head, *How can I be sharing a bed with Robert?* The giggles from Beth and I stilled, as we found each other's face in the dim light shining from the bathroom. For a moment, we didn't say anything, but somehow knew what each other was thinking.

'I don't want to sleep in here,' Beth murmured.

I could see the distress in her eyes. 'Nothing will happen if we say no,' I whispered trying to reassure her. I felt dazed, as I often did when I was with Gina, and my eyes began to feel heavy as I drifted in and out of sleep.

The night became a blur, one minute I was looking at Beth,

and the next it was dark and there was no sign of Beth beside me. I felt confused and rolled over, falling back into a deep sleep.

I drifted into consciousness and I saw Robert's silhouette creeping over the top of me; his head rose from my knees and I could make out he was smiling because his teeth glistened in the night light shining from the weighing room. I watched as he moved his naked body over me, and I tried to blink myself out of some dream to gain some coherent thoughts. Was this meant to be my first time with a man? *It can't be happening this way*, I told myself and tried to move, but my eyes closed, wanting the nightmare to be over.

Robert mumbled something, but I couldn't work out what he was saying, then I felt a sharp pain as he entered me. I groaned, feeling the sensation of his penis move inside me. He started to pant heavily as I lay underneath him, thinking that – with every thrusting move he made into me – I should try to get up and run from the room. But my body felt limp as I fell in and out of consciousness.

I woke at one point thinking it was a bad dream; I wanted to run into my parents' room and wake my dad, like I did as a child when I had a nightmare. I needed to feel safe and be reassured that there were no monsters trying to get me in the night, but this was no night terror; it was reality. I returned to oblivion until my heavy eyes began to wake from my slumber. I was unable to think clearly and tried to retrace what he had done to me. I still had my t-shirt on but no knickers; I was sure I'd not removed them, because I was sleeping in his bed and wanted to make sure I kept them on for some sort of protection, regardless of his rules.

Memories washed over me, and my head started to spin. My eyes darted around the room and I saw that, next to me, Robert was turned away, snoring. I began to weep at the thought of my lost innocence; my virginity had been completely taken away, first by Gina forcing herself onto me and now by Robert, which I clearly hadn't consented to. I could no longer fantasise about my first time being a slow, tender moment with a man I was in love with, telling me everything was fine. And to have the touch of his hands on my body, loving every inch of me, and for me to love him back in the same way. This fantasy had been completely destroyed in one night. Tears stung my eyes. Instead, I had this lump of man snoring beside me. I gulped down my rising sobs and I had a pain in my chest; it wasn't supposed to be like this. I was meant to wake up with the man of my dreams holding me, whispering sweet nothings and stroking my body, making me feel safe. Instead, I felt ruined and worthless.

I crept from his bed and wandered to the bathroom. I checked to see if I was bleeding, but there was no sign of anything. I soaked in the bath, feeling dirty, and scrubbed away his odour. I was in a state of bewilderment. I had grown to look up to these people, yet they had taken the most sacred part of me. I was no longer an innocent virgin, with a choice to keep my virginity. Somehow, this was made to look like I had wanted it all along. Robert would tell me that, when I became successful and made lots of money, Gina and I would travel the world and have the best of everything. I wondered if it was part of my destiny to be with them; I had so many questions in my mind that I gave myself a headache.

Silent tears trickled down my face as I thought of my family; they were there for me, but could only help if I approached them. I couldn't bear to think about telling my parents, or anyone else for that matter, what I had just experienced. I feared that no one would believe me, since I couldn't articulate what had happened during the night; it was fragmented in my mind and the only image that tormented me was his silhouette moving up from my knees. I felt isolated from everyone, and his implied message crossed my mind that he was a man to be trusted and was well respected because he was an ex-police officer. I couldn't compete with that; he would be believed over me. I wiped away my tears and finished bathing. I put a bathrobe round me, ready to sneak from the bathroom, when the door opened, making me freeze.

'Good morning, I've brought you both breakfast in bed,' Gina said, holding a tray with tea and toast on it. She had a knowing expression that turned on a deep rage that was brewing inside me.

I wanted to push the tray into her face because I was stunned by her cheerfulness. From that moment on, my perception of Gina began to change, and the infatuation began to wane.

Robert made me jump by entering the bathroom in that jolly manner of his that I now despised.

I was speechless and finding it hard to believe what had happened; it was all hazy, like a black cloud hanging over me. My sight glazed over, like I was trying to see through fog, but I couldn't piece together the whole night. Just like I couldn't piece together my childhood nightmares; when my father held me close and asked about the terror, I'd just remember the monster coming to get me and then wake up feeling relieved that it was gone. Now I had a real monster standing before me who wouldn't go away, and it was painful to imagine how long he had abused me for during the night.

'Good morning,' Robert said, smiling.

I was lost for words as I stood in the doorway.

'I've brought you breakfast,' Gina added sweetly and approached the bedroom like a dutiful wife.

'Thank you, love, leave it on the bed,' he replied, and walked to the toilet.

I was dumbfounded and blinked as he pulled out his penis – did he think that because he had taken my virginity it was OK for him to wee in front of me? I was swamped with the emotions running through my head and what was happening before my eyes. Robert was making out that the night had been normal and nothing serious had happened. I stood there questioning it myself; was it normal? I thought of Sean and my heart wrenched; why couldn't he have been the one who took my virginity when we tried to have sex? I didn't want to be tormented by my first time, and see the image of Robert moving up from my knees, then over my body and painfully forcing himself into me. I knew Robert wouldn't have kissed my lips, because he didn't like that sort of affection. I was able to take some comfort from not having the taste and smell of him there. I felt trapped in a nightmare with no way of escaping or turning back the clock.

***

I chose to stay silent about my ordeal, fearing the outcome if I was to find my voice. I had to somehow accept the hand that had been dealt to me, and attempt to blank out the night, which was mostly a blur, but was so poignant to the person I was to become. I became very secretive and untrusting, and wouldn't share my deepest thoughts with anyone for many years to come. I tried to focus my mind on something positive to take from it, and the only thing that crossed my mind was that at least I wouldn't have the worry or embarrassment of fumbling under the covers with someone else. Even so, it made me sad to wonder that, if I'd not been raped, who would have been my first love?

I was unable to think of myself as a young girl who was taken advantage of because I was brainwashed and made to think I was a young woman who was willing and game for anything. And Robert could take me any time he wanted, now that he had my virginity. I had grown up quickly, experiencing a world dominated by adults, and Robert being the most dominant figure of all. Even though I was deeply broken, I focused on counting down the days to my trip to Korea. I had the new tear sheets in my book that Satu Models had sent. I missed them, but was comforted by the thought of going back one day.

Reflection

By this time, the grooming process has gone through all the phases, and becomes a matter of the perpetrator sustaining the position he or she is in.

Robert's behaviour in taunting me and tussling me to floor isn't the behaviour anyone should encounter from a mentor; this inappropriate use of force is a violation of one's intimate space. Robert had no regard for me trying push him away, and he persisted in using the power he had to carry through with his agenda of taking my virginity. He fantasised about the girls he chose to stay at his house and who he thought would comply with his sexual demands; those with unpredictable behaviour were kept at a safe distance because he didn't want his cover blown by those he didn't trust to keep a secret. The ultimate sexual violation happened when Robert raped me during the night. I was left completely powerless and confused, because I was drugged into a dazed sleep.

On reflection, I was in denial and I minimised the sexual assault to the extent that it became nothing serious to report. Many victims do this, fearing the consequences; I feared losing my modelling career and that I wouldn't be believed. This was added to the fact that I had witnessed Robert using violence, which made it harder to leave for fear of being beaten. It was far easier to stay with them than to face anyone outside the modelling agency.

If you find yourself in a similar situation, you have to find the faith that you'll be heard and believed, no matter how much you fear the repercussions. You shouldn't let an abuser get away with violating your innocence and freedom of choice. Be brave and find the strength to bring the perpetrators of abuse to justice, otherwise they'll carry on destroying people's lives.

This is what Robert intended when the previous group of girls were growing older, and he needed fresh prey to satisfy his obsession for teenage virgins.

11

LIVING IN TWO WORLDS

Walking through the bustling atmosphere at Gimpo airport in June 1994, I felt fortunate to be travelling internationally with my career. The sordid world I was experiencing back home could be left behind for the time being. I looked at the happy faces of strangers who were preparing for their next journey, and – although I liked my own company – I wondered if I'd always be a lone traveller. It occurred to me that Robert and Gina didn't have me travel with the others who were also chosen to work for the Asian markets. It was like they didn't want me getting too close to the girls without being under their watchful eye. This manipulation through separating me from the others worked, because it stopped me from striking up any conversations about Northern Teen Models when I was alone with them. (Looking back, it was quite remarkable that we never spoke about the experiences we'd had with Robert and Gina, or voiced any violations that may be happening to all of us individually. They had complete control over my life, even though I didn't fully realise it at the time.)

At arrivals, the owner of the modelling agency, Mr Kim, distracted my thoughts as he welcomed me to Seoul. We walked to where the car was parked and got in. Once he drove off, we spoke briefly before I gazed out of the window, and made comparisons between Korea and Japan. I was looking forward to seeing some of the girls, but was soon disappointed when Mr Kim told me I'd be staying at his apartment with him, his wife and a couple from Canada. Gina and Robert sprung to mind, and I wondered if they had something to do with this living arrangement.

***

When we arrived at the apartment, it seemed like the area where I'd be living was quiet and hidden away from the busy streets. After getting out of the car, we went to the apartment, and Mr Kim took me inside and showed me to my room. As I unpacked, I felt a wave of homesickness in the small, muggy room I was given. When I had finished unpacking, I asked Mr Kim if the models' apartment was far, and I demanded to go, even though he wanted me to rest. Mr Kim relented and told me he would take me later that afternoon.

After showering, I sat with the couple and listened as they told me how different Korea was to the Japanese market. It pleased me to hear we were taken by the managers to our jobs as well as castings, though this was only because of the fact that we didn't have working visas and could be deported at any time. They told me a story about officials storming the models' apartment and sending them home, which worried me a little because I didn't want to return to Robert and Gina.

A little later, when we were en route to see the girls, I noticed I had gained more confidence in talking to people since I had got some life experience in the industry and had a few stories to share from my time in Tokyo. I was glad to find that the models' house wasn't far, and I could walk over any time. Amy from Northern Teen Models was sharing the house with five people, including a male model. The house had a lively atmosphere, and I watched enviously as Amy and the others dressed for a night on the town. She asked me to join them, but my bed was calling. Amy found it amusing that I was living with Mr Kim. However, I didn't, believing it could hamper my going out because he could keep a check on me. Amy told me not to be so paranoid. I frowned; I could hardly tell her our mother modelling agency had phoned Satu Models to keep me indoors.

***

The following day, I went straight to the modelling agency to be measured and have Polaroids taken. The modelling agency's office was messy; they had so much stuff and such little space, unlike the spacious rooms and organised chaos at Satu Models.

I breezed through a full day of castings and started to work straight away. I soon felt settled from the waves of homesickness caused by wanting my family. I didn't have time to think; it was all about work. I felt like a rag doll being stretched to the limits of my sanity. The catalogue jobs were brutal in terms of the amount of outfits squashed into one day. It was like I was shooting for two catalogues, but being paid for one. Yet I didn't complain because I simply wanted the experience.

I worked hard, so I played hard whenever I could. We lived in the international district of Itaewon, which is popular for international-cuisine restaurants, shops, bars and clubs. The evenings came alive with locals, foreigners and American soldiers, who were all ready to eat and party.

The girls and I were free spirits, dancing the night away and getting very drunk. Dancing had become a therapeutic outlet for me to release the trauma I had suffered at the hands of my abusers. I felt myself go a little wild, because I didn't have the restrictions Robert put in place. I was like a stray cat, running round late at night, then finding myself sneaking into Mr Kim's apartment as quietly as I could, so I didn't wake up the whole house. I was outwardly free, but inside I was still bound to Gina and Robert when they called to check up on me.

I noticed that, since I was no longer a virgin, I acted more flirtatious with the men who crossed my path, and I wasn't sure if this was a good or bad thing, because they could take me the wrong way. I bumped into Scott, who was a model I'd met in Tokyo on a photoshoot. We chit-chatted before he leant closer to me at the bar and whispered, 'You seem different from the girl I met five months ago.'

I looked at him, puzzled.

'But in a good way,' he quickly added.

Scott then made a pass at me, and – before I knew it – we were kissing.

How nice, I thought, *to be swept away by someone of a similar age.*

'Natasha, when may I see you again?' he said, stepping back from our passionate embrace.

I looked over his shoulder towards Amy, who playfully raised her eyebrows and waved for me to leave.

'I'm out next weekend with the girls, so maybe we could see each other then, if you're out?' I asked.

I didn't want to be alone with a man; I was OK with a kiss, but certainly didn't want to sleep with anyone. Since my experience with Robert, I wouldn't let a man get close, because I'd painted a picture in my mind that some men just used women as sex toys. I was able reel in those I liked for some type of friendship, but then run a mile at the first sign of them wanting more.

***

Approaching the end of my contract, I was booked for a two-day job for a nightwear brochure. The company did the shoot in a penthouse apartment overlooking the city. When I arrived, I looked around in amazement and envied the owners; I hadn't been in any apartment like it before. Elegant archways with long pillars supported the ceiling, and white-and-cream hallways with marble floors led into different rooms. I sat on the sofa in the living room, facing the view of Seoul through the windows, and smiled, counting myself lucky. I was just a girl from Longsight who was now able to see how the other half lived, and this was a living dream that I didn't want taken away.

I daydreamed, while having my hair and make-up done, about how I could achieve having all this. My taste of the finer things in life now meant they were what I wanted to work towards, but – for now – I could live the dream for a few days. Again, I was spoilt and treated like royalty, with the clients providing anything I needed. They took their time creating the right ambience for each garment to be shot; usually, if I were shooting in a studio, I'd be driven nuts by the clients being so particular and wanting them to finish. However, I didn't mind because I was in love with the apartment. They weren't happy with the male model, Bret, and sent him home. I was relieved because, in the shots we did together, he would slip his hands further down the small of my back and make innuendos. This made me feel uncomfortable and paranoid about those men who thought it was OK to touch me and talk to me how they pleased, and I didn't think to put them in their place, as if I lacked some sort of self-worth.

Mr Kim sent his friend Carl to carry on with the shoot. He was nice looking, with a soft Canadian accent and not much experience in the modelling world. We hit it off; however, I was soon disappointed when he mentioned his Korean girlfriend.

We worked until 2am, reshooting, until the clients finally called it a night and asked if I wanted to stay. I grinned, said yes and was soon jumping into the jacuzzi to keep my dream alive, before falling into the fourposter bed and drifting off to sleep.

***

The month flew by. I could have stayed for another month quite easily, but I had to leave and apply for my Japanese visa. Mr Kim asked me to return in the autumn, and I eagerly agreed before he gave me a wedge of dollar bills. I had earned more than in Tokyo, and wondered how much the money was worth in pounds sterling. I had no clue that if I walked through customs with more than the limited amount stated, they would take the money off me. Back then, ignorance was bliss. It was a bonus earning money. I felt I had lived there for free because they advanced everything during the trip. However, I knew I had paid all this back from jobs, but I didn't fully understand how my contract worked, and just went into everything blind and trusted people.

***

On my return from Seoul, Robert took the money and changed it for me, saying he would keep it in his office for safekeeping. However, before he did, he asked me to do something strange, which was to suggest that I take the cash home and show my parents my earnings. Slipping back into obedience, I did what was asked without thinking and put the money down my top for safekeeping until I stepped into my parents' house.

'Hi Dad, look what I've got!' I said, pulling out the wedge of money.

The look of shock on my dad's face said it all. 'What are you doing bringing that home, it should be in your bank account!' he exclaimed.

Instantly, I felt stupid; what was I thinking? Or what was Robert thinking, for that matter? (This behaviour is common for an abuser, and is a way to show people on the outside that being around them is beneficial for the abused. In my case, the amount of money I could earn was sure to make people think I was in good hands.)

***

I always felt on a high during the first weeks at home after a modelling trip, then I'd slide back into the same routine.

Amy returned from Korea and came to the modelling agency.

'Hi Amy,' I said excitedly, and greeted her with a hug.

'Hi Natasha, it's good to see you,' she responded.

We released our embrace.

'How was work for you when I left?' I asked, as Gina and Robert emerged from his office.

'Hi Amy,' they said in sync. I had no chance of getting an answer to my question now that they were in the room.

'How was your trip?' Robert asked.

'Really good; they want me to go back in October,' Amy replied happily.

'Maybe we can go together?' I suggested.

We grinned, knowing we would have so much fun.

'Amy, you and Gina go to her office, and you can tell her

everything about your trip. Cassandra, go and make me a coffee,' Robert intervened, not letting our conversation go any further.

Everyone did as they were told, and I sat in reception feeling rejected.

Amy left an hour later, and I didn't know when I'd see her next. It crossed my mind that we hadn't exchanged home phone numbers, nor had I done that with anybody else, for that matter. Cassandra and I were the only ones staying at the models' house, and Robert suggested we eat out in town.

When we got to the restaurant, I felt a weird vibe from Gina and Robert, and I couldn't work out if I had done something wrong.

'Natasha, we hear you were quite the flirt while you were in Korea,' Robert said, looking menacing and staring into my eyes. 'And you went out of your way to get attention on a night out; we know about the American military base near where you socialised, and Amy went there a few times.' He smiled crookedly, making me feel uneasy.

I hated being put on the spot, and was surprised by his insinuation that I had gone with Amy to the army base. I pictured Amy having this conversation in Gina's office, but knew she wouldn't offer what we had got up to; Gina would have had to probe her with lots of questions.

'Well, yes, we went out. I like to dance and we all got attention,' I said calmly, not knowing what else to say; I thought I shouldn't have to defend myself because I had done nothing wrong. Anyone sitting at the table would have sensed their annoyance at not having control over me while I was away, and – no matter what conversations they had with my Asian agencies to keep me from going out – it just didn't work, and this pissed them off. Travelling to Asia was the only thing that shone a light away from the dark, confusing path my life was travelling along. At the time, I couldn't call it what it was: grooming and sexual abuse.

***

In mid-July, I told Robert and Gina that I was meeting my dad at the pub for lunch and to ask for some money, because I was scared to ask for my own money that Robert was in control of. Robert asked what time I'd be back, and I told him I didn't know. He gave me a phone so they could call if they needed me to return. I ran down to Oxford Street, happy that I could spend some time with my father. I hadn't been with him long when the phone rang to summon me back to the modelling agency. Dad was bewildered that I had to go back so soon, saying that I only had so long for my lunch. (In hindsight, I believe Robert was nervous about me asking my dad for money as it might have caused my dad to question the whereabouts of my pay from Korea.)

***

I flew to Osaka on 25th July. This trip was a failure, even though I was back in Japan. I made up for the lack of work in sightseeing. We lived in a models' apartment in Kobe, which was surrounded by the scenic setting of mountains covered in vibrant greenery. Even though I had a pretty landscape to get lost in, this city seemed far too quiet for a girl who loved buzzing nightlife.

We travelled 25 minutes by train into central Osaka to meet the manager and other models for castings and jobs. The modelling agency had many girls representing them from around the world, and a few of us looked similar, which created competition within the modelling agency. We also had to use the subway and/or walk to all our castings. I wasn't one to complain, but it was high summer and the hot, humid weather didn't make me feel my best on castings. I'd be perspiring, and the make-up I had applied in the morning would have melted away. The only positive I could see was that Eskay Models' models were slim and kept fit, which suited the strict Japanese market that required you to stay thin.

***

I was grumpy, but tried not to show it; however, this was hard because I'd been so spoilt on my previous trips. I couldn't help but compare Osaka to Tokyo. The people in Osaka had a humorous temperament and were less serious than the people in Tokyo. They seemed to joke around, or at least this was the impression I got. I attended many castings, but didn't receive much response from clients, which knocked my self-esteem. Also, I felt that the female manager didn't like me very much. On castings, when she presented me to clients, I sensed she wasn't bothered about managing me. I was sure she made fun of me in front of the clients, because they laughed at whatever she said while they looked through my book. I disliked almost every minute of representing that modelling agency, and it didn't help that there wasn't much to do in the evenings in Kobe.

***

I roomed with two models called Marie and Lucy; we were the youngest and would say goodbye to the others at Umeda train station, knowing they would be partying at some point over the weekend. It felt like we were put there so we wouldn't be tempted to go out. I had to resist the urge to jump on the Shinkansen train bound for Tokyo, and knock on Satu Models' door to let me in.

Living with strangers always opened my eyes. Marie had an eating disorder, and it was outrageous that she was told to lose weight from being a size 10. She spent hours in her room, rather than hanging out with us, especially while Lucy and I ate. She looked frail, but the whiff of sick in the bathroom was the only sign of her issues.

***

The modelling world was brutal at times, with people picking out anything that wasn't perfect. This caused anxiety, and constant worrying about your outer shell and whether you met someone's criteria of what they saw as beautiful. It seemed like there was always something that wasn't quite right, which model agents or clients would pick out. The harshness of the industry made you hard on yourself, and it was frustrating to think that outsiders thought we were comfortable in our skin. But, for many, we were struggling with insecurities from the people who wanted to make us look perfect. Early on in the industry, I learnt to develop a thick skin to people's opinions and judgements, and to let the comments slip by me; however, this was easier said than done. I found a way to focus on the things I liked about my body, and told myself that people didn't have to book me for a job, and what they saw was what they got and it couldn't be changed. I soon realised that the advertising world painted false expectations of what people should try to look like. When I received tear sheets from magazines, my laughter lines and dark circles were airbrushed out, so I looked like a picture of flawless beauty. And, sometimes, if my body was out of shape, it was retouched and slimmed down, so people would buy into a fake portrayal of what they needed to do to achieve this perfection.

***

I felt stuck in Osaka. Gina called frequently, as she knew I was unhappy, and a voice from home made me feel better, even though I wished it was my parents and not the ones I saw as surrogates. When the phone rang, it was usually for the others or it was Gina; I felt like a forgotten child, but understood my family were busy with other commitments. Robert and Gina were clever in using this to their advantage, by being the 'parents' who took an extra interest in what I was doing. This was the emotional support I needed; however, Gina still had me confused and ruminating about our friendship.

She sent me large laser pictures of herself, and told me how much she missed and loved me, only I couldn't return these sentiments with the same amount of passion because it didn't feel right for me to be with a woman any more. Even though it was nice to receive letters in the post, I didn't want pictures of Gina in her underwear. I was fond of her, but didn't miss her in that way. It was just the friendship I missed, and I was grateful she was there when I was low and feeling homesick. I tore the pictures up and threw them away, wondering how I could escape my mother modelling agency.

***

Eskay Models and I began talking about my contract, because I wasn't making enough to cover it. This was the time to think about going home, rather than wasting my time and more modelling-agency money. I had a couple of confirmed bookings, which I had to do, so the modelling agency could recoup what they had lost by having me there – I hated working knowing this. I called my parents, feeling disappointed in myself for not meeting the same expectations as Tokyo and Korea, and I told them I'd be coming home early. After the call, I felt reassured I hadn't let anyone down.

On returning to the apartment after my job, I found Lucy had left me a message saying that Gina had called a few times. I waited patiently by the phone and picked it up straight away when it rang.

'Hi,' I said eagerly.

'Hi Natasha, how are you?' Gina replied.

'I'm OK, I just feel crap working and knowing I won't receive a penny,' I added irritably.

'We have some news that will cheer you up: I've been in touch with Eskay Models and I've looked at flights, and you can come back on the 18th…' Gina paused for a moment. 'We were thinking, Tash, you could come home and not tell your parents which date you're returning, then we can surprise them,' Gina said excitedly.

'Oh, right,' I said, sounding puzzled.

'You can stay with us for a few days to rest, then you can go home feeling refreshed,' Gina added.

It sounded like a good idea at the time, and I went along with their wishes, not knowing what their hidden agenda was.

Reflection

Grooming is a slow, calculated process that ensnares people in a world in which they seem to be a willing participant in the sexual abuse. Perpetrators know that minors with less parental oversight and supervision are more desirable, because they can be coerced easily into complying with their demands. Robert used this knowledge and created a world in which they were meeting one of my needs; this need being extra attention. This is common with molesters, who target children based on family dynamics (such as broken homes, families with mental-health issues and domestic violence); they discover the need, then meet it.

Throughout the grooming process I experienced, Robert always worked on isolating me from others, which further reinforced the connection with them because I had no one to turn to. Gina's attention while I was away gave me the sense that I was thought of and loved, which wasn't being provided by my family at the time. My parents thought I was happy and safe, because I never approached them with any concerns about the agency. All my parents were able to see was how much money I made, and outsiders would assume it was good for me to have Northern Teen Models as an agent because I had the opportunity to travel internationally for work.

Maintaining control at this stage, as Robert did over me, is the aim of most perpetrators, because they don't want to get caught. It became tricky for him when I started to work abroad, which made him step up a gear and try to control my movements while I was away. Robert was skilful in the way he kept me away from the girls at the modelling agency; we were always under his watchful eye and conversations were controlled by him. This is something that is *so* subtle and you can't see it at the time, but this is clear manipulation of your autonomy.

12

ATTEMPTING TO ESCAPE

Gina and Robert greeted me at the airport with open arms, which felt strange because it was usually my parents who were standing there waiting. However, it was good to be back on English soil, even though I was embarrassed by my failure and returning penniless. Robert seemed very chirpy, and he took us straight to the bar for a brandy.

After the second brandy, he said, 'Drink up, we have something waiting for you at the modelling agency.'

I looked at the brandy and slowly sipped it, having a glimmer of an idea of what lay ahead. It crossed my mind to say, 'Take me home,' but I couldn't utter a word and be seen as lying to my parents.

***

An hour later, feeling jet lagged and tipsy, I was at the modelling agency with them. I felt odd as I followed their merry faces into reception. I looked for Cassandra in the deathly silent room, but there was no sign of her. Robert unlocked his office door, and I sat staring at my suitcases, yearning to be home.

'Here's another brandy, you two,' he said handing me one with a cigarette to go with it.

I thought, *I've only been in England a few hours and I'm having brandies thrust upon me with no choice in the matter.* I wondered how I could tell them I didn't want to engage in any more sexual activities with them.

'Tasha, finish your drink and follow Gina into the back room. I've arranged it so she can give you a full body massage; you deserve one after a long flight,' he said, smiling wickedly.

I didn't protest because the thought of a back massage was very inviting. Walking into the back room, I was taken aback; the massage bed was placed in the centre, with towels covering it and a pillow at the end. On the chair beside it lay creams, oils and sex toys. I felt troubled by what she was going to do and my head started to feel hazy.

'Get undressed and lie down, Tasha,' Gina commanded in a bossy manner.

The changing of my name washed over me again; I considered Natasha to be a robot, because I did everything they told me to do automatically. Yet, Claire felt cornered inside me, wanting to break free from their grasp, and these feelings became stronger the more I travelled abroad and had time to reflect. I slowly undressed and wondered why Gina remained clothed. I lay down, and she firmly rubbed cream into my back before massaging briskly.

'Turn over, Tash, and I'll do your front,' Gina said smiling, 'I'm going to put this eye mask over your eyes, so this feels more sensual.'

I turned over and let her blindfold me. I wasn't sure if I liked this new experience of lying on a massage bed, on high display, with my eyes covered to the unknown. I peeped through the mask, feeling scared.

'Don't look,' she said and moved my hand away.

Feeling hot and flushed from the brandy, I began to wonder nervously what lay ahead. I heard footsteps in the catwalk room and they became louder as Robert entered the room.

I froze and thought, *he shouldn't be here.*

Gina placed her hand on my shoulder as if to relax my taut body.

I felt his body brush past the side of the bed.

'It's OK, Tash,' he said, taking my wrists.

Robert tried to tie my hands to the bed, but I broke free. I wanted to take the blindfold off, yet I didn't want to face the full horror of what they were doing. Gina tried to help pin my hands to the bed and failed.

'OK, Tasha, there's nothing to worry about; I won't tie your hands, but you must not move,' he added, leaving the room.

I tried to peep again, but Gina wouldn't let me and held my arm down.

Robert returned, I heard the noise of dishes being put on the windowsill, and the smell of burning wax drifted past my nose.

I screeched as Robert glided ice cubes across my stomach; the coldness sent signals to my brain and my semi-naked body wanted to tense up into a ball. Gina held my hands down, and all I was able to do was wriggle from the sensation.

Robert slid warm knives along my legs and towards my crotch.

I flinched and said quietly, 'No, please stop.'

He carried on and started to drip candle wax on my stomach. I screeched again, but Robert seemed to like the sound of my shriek because he did it again. But this time I forced myself to sit up, releasing Gina's grip, pulled the blindfold off and laughed. This was a laugh to say I was laughing at him and I was making sure he wouldn't ever think he could do this to me. They stood either side staring at me.

'Natasha, you're not ready for this yet,' he said with evil eyes.

I thought, *Never!*

***

I slept heavily that night, which was unusual for someone with jet lag, and I woke the next morning wondering where I was. As my eyes focused on the ceiling of their room, I felt a stab of guilt for not telling my parents I was back in Manchester. The encounters with Robert and Gina started to play on my mind as I saw them differently. I hated feeling stuck inside my body and wanted to disappear. I crept from the bed and snuck from their room to get ready in the top bedroom, where most of my things were stored. I sat on the bed, and the stillness of the moment made me think of ways I could escape. I was itching to get home, but my parents were told I was coming home the following day.

***

We arrived at the office later than usual, and I looked around, yearning to be in Korea where I could work every day.

'Tash, here's your card; go to the bank and check your balance,' Robert said cheerfully.

'OK, thanks,' I replied, taking my card and feeling agitated that it was in his possession. I got in the lift and descended, lost in my thoughts and looking at my name on the card. I had no control over it any more, as Robert had asked me to change my address and have my bank statements sent to the modelling agency rather than home. Robert had started to use my bank account to pay out and receive money from people I didn't know, which I only found out before I went to Osaka.

One morning, I had opened up the office, seen my bank statement and decided to open it. When Robert found out, he went berserk, telling me never to open any mail that came to the office. I felt intimidated and like a child who had their hands slapped for doing something so terrible.

Approaching the bank on Oxford Street, I wondered where the money had gone from Korea. I eagerly put my card in the reader, checked my balance and was pleased to see some money had been transferred into my account. My mood changed; I cheered up about returning empty handed and thought about what I could buy.

When I got back to the office, Robert told me I could keep my card for a while; he gave the impression that he wanted me to think he had given me the money from the goodness of his heart.

***

Late that afternoon, Robert put the phones onto the answer machine, because we were having conversations about the girls and me finding agencies in London. Midway through the talks, the phone rang and it switched to Gina's voice message saying no one can come to the phone right now. My heart skipped a beat as I heard my dad's voice leave a message asking what time I'd be back. I started to panic about him finding out I was home, but calmed down, knowing that my parents wouldn't call Japan.

Gina phoned him back, and it pained me to hear her lie to my father and say I'd be home the following afternoon, and they would pick me up from the airport and drop me off. I wanted so much to be my own person, and pick up the phone and speak to him, but I was stuck. My heart was calling out for an opening in which to be set free, and it was as if my dad could hear my inner voice.

***

The following day, I stood at the front door of my house feeling anxious, wondering who would open the door to my guilt-stricken face. Even though I was welcomed back with love, I felt an unsettling energy in the house, like my family knew I had been back days ago. I stared at myself in the bathroom mirror, and realised I didn't have that 'just got off the plane' look or smell.

I escaped the family chatter, shut myself off in my room and looked out the window to the street I had known all my life. I let my thoughts roam, searching for any answers to those ongoing questions in my head. The more I went away, the more I wanted to be back modelling abroad, even though I got deeply homesick at times and couldn't wait to return home. I was confused by these conflicting thoughts of where home was. Was it with my parents, at the models' house or getting in touch with feeling at home in my own skin? Through the confusion, I could see my growth into the adult world which was already filled with great work opportunities, but contact with others had become a mixed bag of mistrust considering the hidden agenda of what they wanted from me. I looked at my small, unopened suitcase and wondered where my next port of call would be.

***

The summer months were always a time when a lot of girls stayed at the models' house. The older group of models before us, from the late 1980s to the early 1990s, had left the modelling agency; our group was expanding and a newer group forming. I felt squashed, although there was always fun and laughter when we were together.

We had a pampering day on the last weekend of August. Robert and Gina had been to the chemist for fake tan and face masks. The bathrooms were full of giggles, and girls were in and out of the living room, waiting for a shower to become available to exfoliate before applying the tanning lotion.

Robert casually said, 'After all of you've applied the fake tan, come to the living room and wait for it to dry.'

Him saying this felt odd. Gina was the first one in the living room and I wasn't far behind. I sat in my usual chair, which I had acquired for the past few years, and – one by one – girls burst in and sat down with bathrobes or towels round them.

Robert wiggled in with drinks and said, 'You're all girls, so why don't you take off your towels and let the lotion dry properly.'

Gina removed her towel promptly to reveal her breasts; no one said anything because it wasn't the first time they had seen her chest. Like a flock of sheep, we did as we were told, some girls looking more awkward than others, which made us automatically cover our breasts.

'What are you shy of? You're all young women, and I've seen it all before!' Robert added, like he was coaching us to be less self-conscious about our bodies and this was a normal occurrence to happen in his presence.

Wearing just our knickers, everyone repositioned themselves in their seats, trying to relax into the moment.

Whatever was on TV was background noise to what was going on in my head. There was a strong unspoken atmosphere in the room that what we were experiencing was wrong. I took a gulp of brandy, yet with every sip the alcohol was having a sobering effect, helping me see the light of what they had done and said to me over the years. My head started to throb as I thought about his manipulation that caused Gina and me to have a sexual relationship. I shivered, but didn't know if it was my thoughts or the warm brandy hitting my chest. I forgot we were semi-naked when I glanced round the living room; this wasn't normal.

Robert had just left the room, and I noticed one of the new girls was missing and Gina wasn't around either. The others were chatting, but it was like they were miming. I heard footsteps above in their bedroom, and a wave of emotions washed over me, with questions running wild in my mind. Was what they were doing right? After all, we had reached the age of consent and had a choice. Was this abuse of any kind? It couldn't be; I was 17 and should know better. Did they treat us all the same? Had it happened to the others and to the previous group of girls who stayed? It was too much for me to bear as my focus became blurred, making me confused. I pulled the bathrobe over myself and left the living room, wandering up to the main bathroom to get some air.

I sat on the toilet, and heard them chatting with the new girl in their room like they had done with me all those years ago. My stomach sank as Robert opened the adjoining door; he looked a little stunned to find me there. I flushed the toilet and could feel his eyes boring into me.

He stood there with an air of arrogance before saying, 'Oh, what are you doing here? We'll be down soon.'

I felt awkward washing my hands, as my body filled with rage, and I looked straight through him, hearing Gina and the new girl giggling. I couldn't get down the stairs fast enough, and I sat down, wanting to scream and release some emotion. *How dare they do this?* I thought, *Was I to be rejected and pushed to the side because I no longer served their excitement for new prey?*

They entered the living room, light and humorous, while I sat seething in a dark inner world. Robert and Gina picked up on my energy, and Gina approached me, trying to squeeze herself onto my chair. I was tense and made things awkward for her. She displayed an embarrassing show of affection by putting her arm round my shoulder, but this just fuelled my anger as she pushed her semi-naked body against me.

I felt a sudden disdain towards Gina, and I had the strongest urge to push her from me and the chair, so she would fall flat on her face. To think I had let this woman befriend me for all these years; I had looked up to her and been in awe. I felt ashamed with her sitting so close to me, while the others looked on, puzzled. I was annoyed with myself for not letting my true feelings be known by getting up and walking away. I could see what was happening more clearly as I processed my rejection which Gina was trying hard to make up for.

When the tanning lotion had dried, I was relieved to get dressed and go hang out in the garden with the girls. Late in the evening, I sat listening to the banter to block out the turmoil I felt inside. Robert distracted me by giving me another brandy, which was taking effect, accounting for my drunken state.

'Robert, may I go to bed?' I asked, feeling foggy.

'Yes, you're in the top bedroom tonight,' he replied cockily.

It was like I was being punished and banished to the top bedroom, because I was naughty for being in the bathroom unexpectedly. Even though it was a relief, I felt rejected.

I left the living room and walked upstairs to the bedroom. I looked round the room that seemed like mine and thought of my bedroom at home with its empty drawers. I took a deep breath, closed the curtains and jumped into the single bed, so I didn't have to share a double with one of the girls. I lay there thinking, through a haze of alcohol, then stiffened, wondering whose footsteps creaked up the stairs.

I was slightly relieved when Gina opened the door and approached my bed.

'Here are your vitamins, Tasha,' she said sweetly, handing me the tablets. 'Goodnight and sleep well; I love you,' she added.

I was speechless as I watched her leave the room. Tears stung my eyes as the full force of what they had done overwhelmed me again. I thought my head would explode with questions: *Why was I here? How could I get out of this living nightmare? Why did I feel so guilty about thinking of leaving after all they'd done for me?* In my head, I repeated the question, *Who can I talk to about this?* I couldn't open up to my mum; she would be devastated. I sobbed while trying to think of a way I could voice these words to someone. I wanted freedom from this prison, but didn't know how to take flight. I felt scared and very alone – I had no one. I cried myself to sleep, vowing to break free somehow.

***

The following day, I felt ill during the classes: my stomach churned and my body felt weak. At one point, I walked out of the toilet with my face as white as a sheet, and Robert told me to have a rest on the couch in his office. He left the door ajar, and I lay staring at the door and listening to the noise from the other rooms.

Robert came in and closed the door, asking, 'How are you, Tash?'

'OK,' I replied, wanting to be left alone.

He lay with me, stroking my head and talking. I wasn't paying much attention to his words and began to focus on the curtain.

'I'll let you rest for a while; try to have a nap,' he said and then left, closing the door behind him.

I dozed, but the vision of the curtain made my eyes spring open. I glanced round the office. His desk was messy with paperwork and brown pill bottles. Phone wires hung from his table and ran along the floor. The draped curtain was slightly open, and I began to feel nervous at having this much access to his room. My instinct told me to look behind the curtain, but I was too terrified to let my body rise from the couch.

At that moment, Robert opened the door, startling me. 'Are you not asleep yet, Tasha?' he said, smiling and picking up his cigarettes.

'Nearly,' I answered, 'I just woke when you came in.' I felt scared as he left the room. I could hear the girls giggling and talking faintly, because he hadn't closed the door properly. I focused on the curtain again, and by tilting my head I spotted a model's profile poster on the wall and made out a small cabinet. I found it odd that the poster was hidden behind the curtain. Why did he need to keep this part of his room covered? I wanted to look further into my findings, but something told me I wouldn't like what lay behind the curtain.

***

A little while later, Robert suggested I go home and rest. For once, I was happy to comply, and got home as soon as I could.

Even though I was very sick, it was nice to be home and to not feel torn about where I was living. I stayed in the living room, with Mum looking after me, because I was too weak to move up and down the stairs. Mum was worried about the glassy look in my eyes, and began to feel irritated by Gina calling all the time, suggesting that I see their doctor and not my own. Mum told her if I was to see a doctor, it'd be our family doctor. In the end, Mum let the phone ring off the hook. (I believe Robert was worried in case I went to the doctors and did some tests; this would have shown what was in my system at the time.)

***

When I got my strength back after a few days, Mum and I headed into town. We hadn't spent this much time together for such a long time. And yet I couldn't approach her with my darkest thoughts, knowing these revelations would crush her.

***

After spending around ten days at home, it was good to get back to the modelling agency and teach the classes, which gave me something to do. However, it didn't take long for me to feel fed up of pretending to like Robert. I started to make excuses to go home during the week, and – on Sundays – I decided to take extra possessions with me from the models' house to my parents' house. The plan was to disappear without a word, lead a life without them and never revisit the nightmare chapter of my life again.

One weekend, Gina asked why my bags were so full for going to the office. I told her I was taking some stuff home that I didn't wear and was going to give to my cousins, and Gina looked at me curiously. I knew they checked our bags, because I had watched them search a new girl's bag a few months previously. Robert said they checked bags just in case someone stole anything; I was horrified by all of this (in particular, by Gina's questioning) and felt edgy leaving the modelling agency. I couldn't wait to get home and put my things away, and I waited with nervous anticipation for the next time I could take more things home.

***

The following week, Robert irritated me because of his demands on people to serve him like a king, which made me act awkwardly towards him. One day, he told me to go back to the models' house, which pleased me because it was an opportunity to be alone and gather any last bits I'd left lying around.

Later, when Robert and Gina returned to the models' house with Cassandra and a new girl called Annie, I acted relaxed and happy to see them, and blamed my mood on my period.

I couldn't sleep that night, and I worried that Gina or Robert would question me about my bag on the way to the office tomorrow, as it looked bulky because it contained my shoes. However, now I had my things together, I wondered if I could summon the courage to leave without a word. I'd miss the girls, but this was something I had to do.

***

I woke the next morning and sighed; I knew what I needed to do and started to get ready in the first-floor bedroom. I was curious as to why Gina and Robert were arguing on the top floor, and my heart sank when I heard Gina say, 'She took some stuff home last week.'

He went berserk and shouted, 'Tasha, get up here. Now.'

I took a deep breath – part of me wanted to run from the house and never return, but I was too scared – and I walked apprehensively to the bedroom. I found them standing in the middle of the room with the empty drawers open.

Robert's face was like thunder. He screamed at me, 'What do you thinking you were doing, moving your stuff out? Were you planning to leave without a word?' He paused for a moment.

I stood there terrified.

'Who do you think you are? After all that we've done for you!' he shouted.

I stared at them, and Gina looked straight through me.

I thought, *What a bitch for checking the room.* I wanted to rip her head from her neck, as Robert screamed abuse at me. My body filled with anger, and I started to shout back. 'I want to go home; I'm leaving,' I shrieked grabbing my stuff and feeling a fool for making it look obvious that I was leaving by taking bulky bags home.

'You're not going anywhere and you're not leaving the modelling agency,' he yelled, blocking me and staring menacingly into my face. He was like a man possessed and looked like he was going to hit me. His body puffed up and his eyes squinted under a frown that made me feel intimidated.

I stepped back, with tears in my eyes, and picked up my bag.

Robert snatched it, hurting my fingers, and shouted, 'Claire!'

This startled me, as he hadn't called me by my real name since Gina changed it. I liked it, even though I was petrified, and I smirked in defiance with tears rolling down my face, knowing it had struck a chord that I was going to leave.

'Claire, you're not taking any bags from this house,' he said, squaring up to me and making me feel small.

Gina gently took his arm.

'Go and finish getting ready, and wait in the car with the others,' he screeched.

I cried in frustration, desperately wanting my parents.

Robert carried on ranting, 'We've done so much for you, and this is how you want to repay us! How dare you even think about leaving!'

I left the room, feeling scared and humiliated, with Gina following behind.

I went outside and got in the back of the car. I started weeping with Annie sitting beside me. Gina sneaked her hand towards me from the front seat, and I questioned her advance. When all this was her fault, why did this bitch want to comfort me now? I was sure she would remove her hand once Robert joined us. I felt such rage that I wanted to take her hand and crush it. And, as I thought, Gina quickly removed it when Robert approached, his face looking murderous.

Having to listen to his rants made it seem like the longest 30-minute drive into town. I imagined putting my hands round his neck, squeezing hard and not letting go, but I thought twice about risking my own life while he drove. I felt cut off, and – not being able to reach out to anyone – I told myself people wouldn't understand or believe what had happened to me. I felt a strong desire to go back to Asia, thinking that running away was the answer to my living hell. However, this would only help me escape for a while, and then I'd be back in their control when I returned.

Eventually, we reached the modelling agency. I got out of the car and entered the agency in silence; my face was reddened with grief. Annie asked if I was OK, and I smiled through the pain I was feeling. Her reaching out in sympathy made me want to break down. I sat lost in my own world as the girls arrived for the class.

Robert had calmed down and was being nice towards me, which made me feel guilty. This emotion confused me, as I questioned whether my choice to leave them was the right thing to do.

***

I wasn't able to go home that weekend, and – to comply with their wishes – I put some of my things back in the drawers at the models' house. I was made to believe that, without them, I wouldn't have a career. Things settled down after a while, and I was back to sleeping in their room under the watchful eye of Robert.

Reflection

In the time period covered by this chapter, my abuser saw a threat to his web of control when I tried to break free. Sex offenders will do anything in their power to stop the victim leaving, so they can carry on the abuse. Perpetrators use all sorts of emotional tactics, which confuses the victim. Robert was like Jekyll and Hyde, one minute he was ablaze with anger – making me feel intimidated and bad – then he threw me by being kind and attentive, which drew me back into his evil clutches. I had witnessed Robert's aggression and violence, and now it was turned towards me; this left me terrified and crippled, so I was unable to follow through with what was right. I didn't have the emotional or physical strength to stand up to his intense manipulation and violence, because I feared his unpredictability and the threat of him retaliating violently.

I felt helpless, and gave up my need to escape and seek help. This is common among victims; when you feel like you have no control, you tend to give up eventually and accept the fate that's before you. This is the ultimate position the groomer wants you in, they rely on the victim being scared because they're confident of your silence. If you're in this situation, go to the police, even if you feel confused because the abuser has stripped you of everything. You need to break the groomer's cycle and stand tall, so you can break the silence they've pushed you into by speaking out and turning the fear into strength.

13

THE END OF A LIVING NIGHTMARE

In the autumn of 1994, I woke to fierce banging on the front door of the models' house. It was early morning, and Robert shot up to look out of the window. He turned, looking mortified, and said, 'Gina, get up and get dressed.' He hurriedly pulled on his jeans. 'You stay there, Tasha,' he said sternly and left the room quickly with Gina.

The hammering on the front door got louder. I shivered grabbing my bathrobe and got back into bed. My chest began to thump as I heard Robert frantically shouting and making rummaging noises that seemed to come from the ceiling; it sounded like he was throwing things into bags. I froze, looking at the drawn curtains, which were always closed, no matter whether it was day or night. Robert never liked us girls looking out of the windows. I heard muffled shouts at the front door and wondered who it could be at this early hour. The final loud bang came before I heard stampeding up the stairs. I sat holding my knees to my chest in the corner of the bed feeling frightened about the unknown.

A woman entered the bedroom and looked into my distressed face. 'Hello, I'm Detective Jane Wells. Don't be alarmed; please get up and put some clothes on,' she said gently.

I did as she asked, then I walked to the landing towards the commotion and saw the confusion on the other girl's faces, all of whom were unsure of what was going to happen next.

Some of the officers left with Robert and Gina, and the remaining officers searched the house.

'Quickly gather your stuff; Robert has given me the keys and asked us to go to modelling agency,' Cassandra said hastily.

The officers left with bags, and we followed soon after at a fast pace and went to the train station, led by Cassandra.

***

We arrived at the office, and I sat stunned in reception, as Cassandra unlocked Robert's office, went straight to the curtain and opened it. She started throwing video cassettes, photographs and a video camera into a black bin bag.

At 12.30pm, detectives raided the office. They took boxes filled with items from Robert's office and the bag Cassandra had started to fill. Everything was happening so fast that I didn't know what to think.

Gina was released on bail later the same day and came to the modelling agency distraught, telling us to go home, to not say anything to our families and she would ring us with any news about Robert. I went home in a daze and acted as though nothing had happened.

***

One week after the raid, news of it became public knowledge. A local newspaper printed the story, alongside a picture of Robert and a police hotline number to call with any information. A detective had said, 'We want to hear from any parent who has taken their daughter to this place.'

This eruption began when two sisters under 16, complained to their mum about Robert. She phoned the police to say her daughters had been victims of a sexual assault. I was curious who the girls were, and I worried about what people would think of me, because I was 17 and hadn't said anything.

***

Robert was released on bail, and I returned to a ghostly office. I felt the loss of my friends who had left the modelling agency, and I had no way of getting hold of them. Cassandra and I were the only girls left, and Robert kept telling us that he had done nothing wrong.

***

I ignored the news, not wanting to face the truth of what he had been doing for years, and chose to remain with them, believing his words. My parents asked if I'd experienced anything untoward, and I denied anything they thought might have happened and told them everything in the news about Robert was a lie. They seemed to believe me; I had neither the strength nor the courage to tell my parents about the last couple of years. Friends in my community asked if Robert and Gina had interfered with me in any way, and it horrified me that people I grew up with might find out, so I told them they were false allegations. (Unbeknown to me – following the newspaper story – a major incident room was opened at a police station, with phones to answer the many calls now flooding in from the public about Northern Teen Models.)

***

I sat with Gina, Robert and Cassandra at the usual table in the Chinese restaurant when things seemed to have settled down. I looked at the empty spaces and thought of the girls I had been friends with for three years. I felt a deep sadness as I thought of the fun times and wondered whether I'd see them again.

Robert soon broke my reverie by saying, 'Tasha, what do you want to do? You may stay with us or go to Korea.'

I looked into three staring faces.

'I'd like to go to Korea again,' I replied, feeling relief at the thought.

'I had a feeling you might say that. Maybe you could go for a couple of months this time and all this mess will be sorted out by the time you get back,' he said confidently.

I looked at Cassandra and wondered what she would do now that the modelling agency was desolate.

***

The following day, Gina phoned the agency in Korea and prepared my contract. I was happy to run away and block everything from my mind, although part of me knew that my problems were still going to be there when I returned, only not how I imagined. My parents were surprised when I told them I was going to Korea the following week; they didn't say what they were thinking and went along with my wishes.

During this last week at the modelling agency, Robert must have been feeling optimistic, because he decided to buy new carpets throughout the office and rearranged the furniture. I wondered about his motives, because no one phoned apart from the many furious people leaving messages, shouting pervert or paedophile.

Robert was incensed about the abusive calls; he got up from his chair and deleted the latest message shouting, 'I've done nothing wrong, and if I go down for 10 or 20 years, I'll make those girls suffer for the damage they're causing.'

The venom in his voice kept me still in my seat. The energy in the office was tense.

Then, Robert said, 'Tash, I have to tell you something, and what I'm going to say is something I had to do to protect Gina; it has nothing to do with what is going on now.'

I lit a cigarette and blew out the smoke nervously.

'I had to make a video recording when you and Gina were in the back room,' he stated.

I sat there wondering how this could be possible.

He continued, 'The reason we did this was that the previous model Gina slept with tried to accuse her of sexual assault.'

I stayed mute, not understanding the full extent of his confession. (I believe Robert told me this to soften the blow of Gina being charged with indecent assaults against young female models, yet he had no remorse for my being so brainwashed by them and being made to think I wasn't a victim of his perverted world.)

***

I breathed a sigh of relief as I boarded the plane bound for Korea. I was alone with my thoughts for the next 14 hours, and something told me I wouldn't see Robert or Gina again. I felt very confused about defending them, and guilt-ridden for not being completely honest with my parents. Fleeing to another country was the only way I could see out of this mess, and I was optimistic that it would have sorted itself out when I returned. Memories and conversations swirled round my mind as I tried to sleep, but I stared at the chair in front of me and wished the person next to me would stop trying to make small talk, because my head was pounding. I loathed myself and was scared of what people might think; I didn't want people to judge me for staying as long as I did, with everything that went on, and for not uttering a word about Northern Teen Models.

***

Mr Kim picked me up from the airport, and told me I was staying with him again and that I'd have the bigger room.

'Amy is back too; she came with another Manchester modelling agency,' he eagerly told me.

'Really, that's great. I can't wait to see her,' I replied. Hearing this news lifted my spirits, yet I was afraid of any discussions we might have about Robert. All I wanted to do was keep what I'd experienced to myself, try to erase the most recent chapters of my life and not revisit them ever again.

***

When Amy and I met, we happily embraced. We talked about the fun times at Northern Teen Models, and I purposely avoided the encounters with Robert and Gina, because I wasn't brave enough to bare my soul. I was thankful that I had no time to think about what may be brewing in Manchester, because I was kept busy with castings and work, and lived for partying at the weekends.

***

One evening, the girls and I headed out early, and I was about to find out how much alcohol my body could store without falling to the floor.

Sometime later, my head started to spin, and I felt unable to follow on to the next bar, so I started to stomp off in the opposite direction towards the apartment. Amy and the others shouted after me, and I glanced over my shoulders to wave them off.

All I remember was turning briskly to walk up the hill, and then briefly coming back to consciousness hearing a man's voice say, 'What do we have here?' My vision narrowed and I was in oblivion again.

***

The next morning, I woke to a knocking on the door. My eyes flickered open and I focused on my surroundings; this wasn't the room in Mr Kim's apartment. Standing at the door was a tall Jamaican man who was speaking Korean to someone who didn't sound pleasant. I looked down and patted myself; I was fully clothed. I tried to gain some coherent thoughts of the night before, and all I pictured was waving at Amy, the spin up the hill and a man's voice. I began to feel panicked because I couldn't remember any more, so I leapt from the bed in the corner of the tiny room and grabbed my shoes.

The man turned and tried to calm me down by saying in a strong American accent, 'Everything is all right, honey. I found you. You were passed out on the ground, and I didn't know where to take you because you were unconscious.'

My body was in flight mode, and I was gone from the room without uttering a word.

I stood in the street for a moment trying to get my bearings, then I started to run, like a wild prey animal running from its predator. I slowed down, reckoning I'd run far enough, and stopped to ask someone the direction of the Hyatt Hotel. They pointed in bewilderment at my frantic state, and I started to run again until I found myself on familiar streets. I ran past one of the other models as they said good morning; I was so distressed that I didn't realise I knew them.

Eventually, I reached the apartment. There was no sign of movement when I entered it. I locked myself in the bathroom and took a long shower, wondering if the stranger had touched me in my unconscious state, but everything seemed OK. I went to my room, locked the door and lay in bed, searching my mind and body, and wondering if I'd been raped. I felt so lonely and afraid, and I decided to phone Gina, even though I was terrified they might scold me, but I had to tell someone that I had blacked out and didn't know if anything had happened to me.

I made the phone call, and the tears rolled down my face as I tried to articulate what had happened the night before.

Gina passed the phone to Robert.

'Calm down, Tasha. We can't do anything now, but we'll speak to Mr Kim,' he said firmly.

'But he isn't here,' I screeched.

'Just be calm,' replied Robert, 'We'll call you tomorrow. Try to have a nap, OK? Goodbye.'

The line went dead.

***

The next day I woke to the phone ringing; it was a call from Gina's sister informing me that Gina and Robert were no longer allowed to contact me.

I could hear Gina crying in the background saying, 'Be strong, stick it out over there and tell someone about Saturday night.' I sat with the receiver in my hand, fearing something was seriously wrong at home. (I wasn't to know this would to be my last contact with them.)

***

The following weekend, I scarily, but luckily, bumped into the man who had picked up my unconscious body from the street. He apologised for frightening me, but explained he couldn't wake me to ask who I was and that girls had been having their drinks spiked. I shook my head in embarrassment for being so careless, thanked him for helping me and said I was sorry that I ran away. I decided to head back to the apartment because I was paranoid about repeating the same experience.

When I returned to the quiet apartment, I received a phone call and was surprised to hear my mum's voice demanding that I came home. I told her I wasn't able to break my contract. The cracks in her voice unsettled me, though she was being firm and telling me to inform the modelling agency that I had to return. I came off the phone feeling unsure of the demands being made of me, as my parents had never acted this way before. The modelling agency was baffled when I wasn't able to explain why I had to leave so abruptly, and told me I couldn't break my contract.

***

That night, I was wide awake when I climbed into bed; my mind was fuzzy and working overtime as I brooded about what was going on back home. I tossed and turned all night, and woke up from a restless sleep feeling deeply upset. I really needed to call my mum later in the day.

When I called her, Mum wasn't happy with me telling her I had to stay; she started to weep and put my aunt on the phone.

'Hi Claire; please, you have to come home now,' she stated, her voice sounded clear and firm.

'I can't,' I replied, 'The modelling agency told me I have to stay because I have jobs booked.'

The silence between us unnerved me.

'Claire, you have to get home, because your brother has been in a car accident,' explained my aunt.

I was stunned as I stood there holding the receiver. 'Really? Is he OK? What happened?' I asked, trying to gather as much information as possible.

'He is in hospital, and you need to get home as soon as you can,' she said softly.

I was thrown, but not convinced. We said our goodbyes, and I hung up, wondering why my parents couldn't speak to me and tell me such devastating news about my brother, and why they hadn't told me on the first phone call. Somehow, my instincts knew they were lying.

***

When I went to the modelling agency the next day, I told them I had to go home as soon as possible. They weren't happy, but my booker reluctantly checked for early flights, though there were none available until the following week.

I called Mum and she pleaded with me to get home. I was curious why she hadn't mentioned my brother in this conversation; I felt muddled and didn't really know what to think any more.

Later that afternoon, Mum called to say she had booked me a ticket on the next flight home, but with a different airline. I was annoyed when I hung up the phone and disappointed to be leaving, because the work would have been plentiful, and now I was leaving with no money again.

***

A whirlwind began. I didn't know whether I was coming or going when I told my booker the flight details Mum had given me.

'Are you sure that's the correct time?' she asked, looking confused.

'Yes, that's the time I wrote down,' I replied, trying to read her face.

'We can't take you to the airport tomorrow evening, you'll have to take the coach,' she said, still looking puzzled.

'That's OK,' I replied, feeling rejected and knowing they were annoyed with my sudden departure.

***

The following evening, I said my goodbyes and told the modelling agency I was sorry to be leaving so early. Amy and I dragged my suitcases up the steep road to the Hyatt Hotel coach pick-up point.

When we arrived at the pick-up point, Amy hugged me and said, 'I hope your brother will be OK. Let's meet up when I return.'

'Thank you for helping me with my cases. See you back in Manchester,' I replied, and then I got on the coach. I found a seat, sat down, looked from the coach window at Amy's smiling face and waved. It wasn't long before the coach drove off.

An hour later, I arrived at the airport. It was dark as I gathered my stuff and it seemed quiet, apart from the many businessmen leaving. Something didn't feel right as I walked towards the entrance. A security guard stood at the sliding doors.

'Hello,' I said trying to walk in.

'The airport is closed; no more flights today,' he replied.

'But I have a flight leaving tonight,' I said, feeling a little panicked.

'No departures tonight; come back in the morning,' he stated and half-smiled, not saying anything else.

I walked away, having flashbacks to my booker's confused face, and kicked myself for not double-checking the flight details. I found a phone booth and searched my purse for some change. Glancing to my right, I saw a Korean man looking at me, which made me feel defensive. I turned, making sure the door was shut, and phoned home.

Mum answered, sounding brighter.

'Hiya Mum, will you check the flight time? I think you've given me the wrong one,' I said softly trying not to sound panicked. I heard Mum shuffling through papers, and I looked out the window to darkness and noticed the man was still standing there; I thought he seemed pleasant enough.

'Oh God, I'm sorry; I've given you the wrong time. You leave in the morning,' Mum said, sounding distraught.

'Don't worry, I just need to get some more change to call the modelling agency and see if they can pick me up, then I'll call you back,' I confirmed. I picked up my bags, ignoring the Korean man, who was now approaching.

In broken English, he asked, 'Where are you flying to?'

'England,' I replied, trying to sound confident.

'No international flights tonight – in the morning. Where did you stay here?' he asked with a concerned look on his face.

'I stayed in Yongsan-gu,' I replied, wondering where the conversation was leading.

'Oh, it's too far for me to go. I live near here, you may stay with me and my family. I'll bring you back in the morning. My name is Kyu,' he said sincerely.

My gut feeling told me he was safe, and I decided to trust my instinct.

'I'm Claire; it's nice to meet you,' I replied, and I was surprised I'd used my real name.

We walked to his car and loaded my cases into the boot.

For a split second I thought, *Should I be doing this?*

We communicated with broken English and gestures as he drove, and talked about our family members. When we arrived at his apartment, Kyu asked me to wait in the car while he told his wife he was helping me. He got out and headed to his apartment.

A short time later, I watched Kyu approach the car, and was relieved when he told me to take the stuff I needed for the night and leave the rest in the boot.

I did as he suggested, and we walked to his apartment. I felt at ease when he opened the door to his cosy apartment, and introduced me to his wife and two children. They were very polite and welcoming. The kids looked at me wide-eyed; I don't think they had met many foreigners and especially one standing before them in their home. I tried talking to them, but much of what we said was lost in translation, and so we relied on body language and smiles.

Kyu told me I could use his phone to call home. When they heard my voice, my parents were relieved and asked me to thank Kyu profusely.

Kyu gave me his and his wife's bedroom. Even though I protested and told him the couch was fine, he insisted that I take it.

That night, although I lay in a stranger's bed, I felt safe and was soon asleep.

***

In the morning, my alarm buzzed, making me jump from a solid slumber. I heard faint sounds and the smell of breakfast. Opening the door to the living room, I smiled at Kyu's wife and children. 'Good morning,' I said warmly.

They bowed, and Kyu motioned me to sit facing him at the breakfast table. I didn't know what else to say because we had already talked as much as we could. I sat contently and admired the man who gave a stranger a safe place to sleep for the night. His wife placed a Korean breakfast in front of me, 'Kamsahamnida [thank you],' I said, bowing with gratitude, and tucked into the noodle broth as the children watched my every move.

Half an hour later, I was saying goodbye and thanking his wife for her kindness.

As promised, Kyu drove me safely back to the airport. When we arrived I repeatedly thanked him for helping me. He bowed and gave me his business card.

***

I felt sombre as my flight landed at London Heathrow.

Wondering about the unknown of what to expect when I arrived home made me feel anxious. I smiled at the air hostess, and stepped off the plane to find my dad standing on the jet bridge. I was taken aback, and knew something wasn't right, given that my father was meeting me in London and not Manchester. My stomach ached as I saw pain in my father's dark eyes, and even though he smiled I knew it wasn't my brother's pain I could see – it was mine. We embraced, and I looked over his shoulder, locking eyes with a woman who was standing there scrutinising me. Walking from the bridge, I wondered why she was following close behind.

Feeling irritable as we approached flight connections, I angrily said, 'Dad, who's that?'

'Claire, it's a police officer,' Dad said and paused. 'This isn't about your brother,' he continued, taking a deep breath.

I looked at him as he explained why they had to lie to me.

'I'm sorry, but we had to say your brother had an accident as we needed to get you back, that's why we had to say something happened. The police were afraid they would intercept you from your original flight.'

'Who?' I asked.

'Robert and Gina,' confirmed my dad, 'The police came to our house to speak to us about the modelling agency.'

The realisation hit me like a ton of bricks, and I stormed off screeching, 'Get her away from me.' I was overwhelmed with a mix of emotions, and rage filled my body from knowing my parents were aware of what I'd experienced. I felt totally exposed and needed space; I couldn't bear the officers near me.

'Claire, we have to return with them. They're making sure you get back home safely; they're nice people,' Dad said trying to calm me.

The officer respected my wishes and joined the other plain-clothed police officers, while Dad and I found a quiet place to talk.

It broke me having to watch my father's anguish at trying to find words to express what he knew. Tears stung my eyes as I watched his well up too.

Fighting back the tears, he said, 'We had to get you on another flight, as we thought we wouldn't be able to get you back with us.'

I sat there silent.

'Your mum and I thought it best that I came, because she didn't feel strong enough to meet you here; she is too upset.' Dad adjusted himself before carrying on, 'Your mum and I were taken to the police station to look at some videos.'

The distress in his eyes hurt my heart, and I began having flashbacks to my first day in the changing room, then to Robert's office with the draped curtain and Cassandra throwing tapes into bin bags. Tears rolled down my face as I began to piece everything together, along with Robert's confession before I left.

'Mum and I were sat down at the police station, and shown a video of you and Gina. We had to identify it was you,' he said as tears trickled down his face, which I couldn't bear since I hadn't seen him cry before.

I felt guilt-ridden because I was the cause of his pain.

'Your mum had to look away as soon as she had identified you from the earrings you wore,' Dad stated and took my hand. 'I carried on watching the screen and witnessed you being sick.'

Tears burnt my cheeks as I cried uncontrollably at the thought of my parents' suffering, and I sobbed in my father's arms.

'We had no idea; I'm so sorry, Claire,' he said holding me tight.

The thought of my dad having to see his little girl's innocence taken crushed me. I sunk deeper into our embrace, too completely choked to find words. My throat and chest hurt from never having cried so much. Pulling back, I looked ahead to find a middle-aged couple were trying not to look concerned about what they were witnessing.

Changing the subject to Kyu, Dad said, 'We were having kittens when we found out there were no flights in the evening.'

I smiled through my torment. 'I've got his business card, so I can send him something in the post,' I replied.

'There are some good people out there. We're lucky you found him,' confirmed Dad.

We sat for a while, watching the world go by and finding the strength to gather ourselves before we flew to Manchester.

***

During the flight, the detective sat next to me. Even though I was wary of her, I still entertained her small talk as she asked me questions about modelling in Asia.

***

When we finally returned home, the officers said they would be in touch to take my statement. Mum opened the door, looking distressed, but she hugged me close. I was too exhausted to shed any more tears.

I was glad nothing more was discussed, but there seemed to be a portent in the air, waiting for someone to make the first move. As I went upstairs and unpacked, I knew the first move wasn't going to come from me.

That night, I lay in bed wide awake, yet I was feeling lighter from not carrying the burden of my ordeal alone any more. However, my parents and the police only knew the half of it. The anguish I had just experienced with my father wasn't going to make me talk about the last three years, because the shame and guilt were too overwhelming. I felt vulnerable and exposed as I drifted into a light slumber, wondering what was going to happen next.

Reflection

Grooming distorts the victim's mind, and once the abuser has full control there isn't much behaviour you're going to question. I didn't understand that I had been groomed and that what had happened was *actually* abuse, which is why I remained in contact with them and denied everything when questioned.

This was where Robert manipulated my thoughts further, by making me think the charges against him were false. When a sex offender is unmasked, they act like they've done nothing wrong. Their regret is from getting caught, and they regard themselves as innocent because of the inevitable consequences they must face. Robert knew what he had done was wrong, yet he had no remorse, since his warped way of thinking saw his victims as fair game because most girls were at the age of consent for sex.

As I analysed my teenage self and researched grooming, I came across *Stockholm syndrome*, which was something I could relate to and helped me begin to unravel the effects of grooming. I had formed a bond with Gina and Robert and had positive feelings towards them, which – because of the emotional stability they gave me – impeded my ability to see the reality of my experience.

However, I couldn't label myself as a victim and accept that I needed help to make sense of my feelings and the situation I was in. It's only now, as an adult survivor, that I'm able to see the pattern of grooming unfold before my eyes as I've written my story. I had mixed feelings when what had happened to me became exposed to the people I loved, and I hated the fact I was the cause of their pain. I was left guilt-ridden and ashamed, blaming myself for everything, and the only thing I could do moving forward was to shut people out and close the door on the chapter, until I was ready to face the unfinished business and make peace with it. If it has come this far for you, then this is where you need to seek therapeutic support to allow you to process the experience and heal.

14

POLICE STATEMENT –
THE AFTERMATH

During my first week at home, a police officer called Sharon came to take my statement. My family left the house while I talked to Sharon about Northern Teen Models. I sat facing her with a pillow on my knees. To begin with, her questioning was sensitive. I spoke in detail about the weekend classes and the work I did at the modelling agency, before nattering about Japan to avoid exploring the sexual assaults. Sharon seemed puzzled by my skirting around the aim of why she was there, and asked why I was still defending them by not saying anything.

The more she pushed with leading questions, the more I shut down, and I brought my knees close to my chest as if to protect myself from the outside world. It was obvious where she wanted to lead me to. I knew she had watched my ordeal on the video they had made my parents watch, but I couldn't open up and sell my soul to someone who was probing and rushing me.

'Claire, I'm going to show you some videos and pictures,' Sharon said, reaching for her bag.

I showed her where the video cassette recorder (VCR) was, and remained standing while she pressed play.

The tapes showed Gina enjoying intercourse with various businessmen, and the final video showed her winking at the camera. I looked away, not needing to see any more because it made me feel sick.

'Gina isn't so innocent, Claire,' Sharon added with slight irritation.

She showed me another video, but this time my stomach churned as I watched myself lying dazed in Gina's arms before I threw up. My heart wrenched at the thought of my parents having to endure seeing this tape. The pain was unbearable, and I felt deeply guilty for putting them through this torture. I had no regard or compassion for the 17-year-old whose youth had been stolen. I found it easier to suppress it all and push the stupid, naive girl from my mind. Yet, what she really needed was someone to say it wasn't her fault and she wasn't to blame. Sharon overloaded my capacity to think straight. I wanted her to leave me alone because I was feeling emotionally exhausted and overwhelmed. However, she kept pushing.

'Here are some pictures, Claire, which you may find distressing, but I need to show them to you so you can see what they were secretly doing,' she said.

I sat down as Sharon passed me the pictures, one by one. They showed that girls' nightdresses had been pulled up on various occasions (at sleepovers at the models' house), exposing female genitals. I closed my eyes for a moment in the hope that this living nightmare would be over. I had no clue that Robert had created so much grief for many girls. I took some comfort from the fact that others were going through the same suffering. My mind ticked over as I relived the abuse, but I couldn't bring myself to talk and piece the years of grooming together.

'Claire, if you're worried about going to court, I can assure you that you won't have to see them while giving evidence,' Sharon confirmed.

I sat there stunned, holding the pictures, and feeling disgusted and broken.

'A screen can be placed around the witness box, so you don't have to face them, and you'll be with the other girls, so you can support each other,' she added.

I didn't like to feel coaxed; I had suffered enough of that to last me a life time.

'Is there anything else you wish to add to your statement?' Sharon asked, seeming exhausted by my lack of elaboration in my story.

'No, I don't think so,' I replied.

'If there's anything else you need to say, please contact me and I'll come here rather than you having to come to the station,' said Sharon as she gathered the evidence and returned it to her bag, giving me the impression her patience had run low. Before leaving, Sharon turned to face me. 'Do you want to see a counsellor?' she said in a matter-of-fact way, like it wasn't essential for me to see one.

'No, it's OK,' I replied, not really understanding what a counsellor actually did.

She walked to the front door and opened it, telling me she would be in touch if she needed to ask any more questions. I smiled as I watched her walk to her car and disappear into it. Once she had gone, I closed the door, stood with my back against it and sighed, feeling glad she was gone before I had a meltdown.

Everything ending so abruptly – compounded by Sharon's lack of understanding and compassion, and her not taking my needs and feelings into consideration – created an invisible fortress around me. This was to stop people getting close to me. I was determined (to my own detriment) that no one would chip away at this stone wall in a hurry. I didn't want to talk because I didn't understand what had happened to me. I needed a safe space in which to realise I had been groomed, abused and raped of my innocence by two people I had grown to love. It was going to take a long time to begin to untangle the web of psychological manipulation they had created. I was deeply traumatised, and it'd take all the courage and strength I could muster to help myself heal from the wound.

***

A week before Christmas, Mum asked whether I'd carry on modelling. Despite what I had experienced, the modelling career I had mapped out in the Far East was a good experience, and I couldn't bear the thought of losing that. My friends had moved to different agencies in Manchester, and I needed to do the same. I made a phone call to Image One Models and told them I was looking for another modelling agency. They invited me to come in for an interview the following day, which lifted my spirits. I certainly didn't want to sit around feeling sorry for myself – I had to move on, and not let those two people ruin my present and future life.

Even though I was now settled at home, my sleep was disrupted. I lay awake before sunrise on the day of my interview, gathering my thoughts about the next path I was about to take and wondering what to expect from another Manchester modelling agency. What niggled the most was how they would react as a result of knowing where I had come from.

Mum accompanied me to Image One Models. We barely spoke a word on the bus into town. It was only four years ago that I had taken the same bus journey with Leanne and Barbara, feeling excited. This was more of a sombre affair; so much had happened that I felt much older than my 17 years. Glancing to my right, at Mum sitting beside me, I wondered if things would have been different if she had been by my side the first time. I gulped back the pain, as somehow I knew the outcome would have been the same because of the facade Robert displayed.

As we walked through town after having got off the bus, thoughts of Northern Teen Models filled my mind. I held my portfolio close to my chest, like I was holding the traumatised adolescent and not letting her fall apart. I felt sad because part of me was still attached to where my career began. I couldn't turn back the clock and change things into a happy fantasy; I needed to accept the reality of the person I had become from my experience. I focused on the good times I had shared with the girls and the classes that had laid a good foundation for becoming a professional model.

When we reached Image One Models' office building and walked in, I came face to face with a gated lift and began to have flashbacks of entering Northern Teen Models for the first time. The curtain, Robert peering over his glasses with a glint in his eye as he held my interview form, and the encounters in the back room washed over me. I pushed the thoughts from my mind and told Mum we should take the stairs to the third floor.

When we reached the booking office, we were greeted by friendly faces, but I was paranoid that they were being overly nice because they knew where I came from. My stomach churned when I locked into a gaze with Elaine, the old head booker at Northern Teen Models. I felt transparent, like she could see straight through to the dark truths that lay behind my eyes.

The director of the modelling agency, Heather, showed Mum and me to her office, and offered us seats in front of her desk.

Heather began to talk and looked through my book; she had a lovely, warm presence. However, I held my cards close to my chest so no one could hurt me. Heather complimented my pictures and told me she would love to have me on her books.

'Claire,' she said gently and paused.

I met her gaze, wondering about the tone of her voice.

'Do you still want to keep your model name?' she asked.

I froze and was transported back in time to when my name changed; I hated having flashbacks and blinked to get rid of them. My head told me to keep the model name; however, my heart said lose it. I wondered how my agencies in Asia would react, but it was my reaction that was the strongest. I didn't want people asking questions about why I had changed my name in the first place, and I wasn't brave enough to face my past just yet.

'I'll have to keep it,' I said, looking towards Mum for any input on the matter, 'They know me as Natasha and I don't want to confuse them.'

I hadn't given much thought about my name and felt bad for keeping it. Yet, it was far worse to think about being put on the spot about where my name came from; at least this way I could hide behind it. It felt tense in the room, with many words unspoken, and I was relieved that Heather changed the subject. I wondered for a split second whether finding another modelling agency so soon was the right thing to do.

'What would you like to do next? Do you want to travel to Asia again?' Heather said as she closed my book. 'Or do you want to become established with work here in Manchester? And there's Europe to think about in the future,' Heather said enthusiastically.

This all sounded exciting and nothing like what I was told at Northern Teen Models. Sitting in front of Heather was a comfort because the modelling agency felt legitimate. Although, I tortured myself with 'if only' and how different things could have been if I'd set foot in their direction instead. Then I wouldn't be wary of people and nervous of giving eye contact for fear of them seeing the core of my grief and working out my past story. Grief wasn't a place I wished to explore any time soon.

'I'd love to go back to Tokyo; Satu Models wanted me to go next month,' I said feeling happier that I could escape again.

'OK, I'll get in touch with Satu Models, let them know you're here and have them send over a contract for January,' Heather concluded, then she stood up, smiled and led us from her room and into the booking office where everyone welcomed me to Image One Models.

At the age of 17, life can begin for some, perhaps finding their first job and having more responsibilities. Late teenage years are an exciting time, due to having more freedom; however, I had lived and seen more than many my age, and I wasn't sure if that was a good or bad thing.

Elaine walked us from the booking office to reception, which made me feel anxious. 'If you ever need to have a chat about anything, all you have to do is let me know and I'll be here,' she said sincerely.

I felt she knew more about what I had been through, and this made me feel exposed. Northern Teen Models had left me feeling that I couldn't trust anyone, because I always wondered about their agenda and what they wanted from me. I had lost my ability to speak frankly, and I was terrified of being judged by people, who would form an opinion and may gossip about me.

'Thank you, Elaine' I replied, knowing full well I wouldn't utter a word to anyone.

As I walked out of the modelling agency with Mum, I was choosing to close the curtain and not revisit the nightmare pages again. My guard was up and I focused on my career because it was the only thing that would keep me sane.

***

I wasn't asked to testify against Robert and Gina. I knew this would be the case because my statement wasn't sufficiently detailed about the sexual abuse to send them to prison.

In the time leading up to the three-month trial two years later, I had completely shut down. During that time, I chose not to read anything in the papers or switch the TV on for the local news. The beginning of my teenage years were closed chapters until the time came for me to explore them with more understanding and knowledge about grooming.

In 1996, Robert was jailed for 20 years. He was originally charged with more than 60 sex offences, but the number was reduced to 17, which is the maximum a jury may hear in one case. He was convicted of six rapes, five indecent assaults and three charges of taking indecent photographs (even though he had taken hundreds of secret photographs of children under 16).

When the judge read out his sentence at Manchester Crown Court, Robert turned to the public gallery and winked at his new girlfriend before being led away in handcuffs to begin a life behind bars. Pleading she was a victim, Gina was found not guilty of all four of the indecent assaults she was charged with, three of them jointly with Robert.

At the time, the case was one of the biggest ever police inquiries in Greater Manchester, and they found him to be one of the most prolific sex offenders ever to come before the courts.

The judge told Robert, 'The parents of these girls trusted you and relied on you to look after their daughters. In some cases, they were well under the age of 16. You raped them to try to satisfy your evil lust. Some of the victims are still receiving counselling and some may never live normal lives again'.

Robert's 20 years of grooming vulnerable teenagers in groups was over; if he hadn't been caught, he would have carried on brainwashing girls with praise, punishment, affection and violence until he had a group that would comply with his sexual demands. It's terrifying to think how many other lives he could have destroyed had the two sisters not approached a safe person.

I believe there's safety in numbers; however, the final group of girls Robert and Gina groomed were all singled out and made to feel special, which controlled what we spoke about. The sisters had each other to talk to, and my guess is they had used each other's strength to speak out. I didn't trust my inner voice, which had heard the alarm bells ringing from the beginning and been telling me things weren't right. If we're taught to listen to those whispers, to not suppress them and to trust our intuition, we could find ourselves living in a different future.

Joining the links

'If you ever find yourself in the wrong story, leave.'
– Mo Willems

I introduced this book with questions of 'Who am I?' and 'Why am I here?' These questions now lead to 'Who am I after completing the circle of unfinished business?' My story began with a curious mind that was wondering, *What lies behind the curtain?* and ended with many shattered lives when it was unveiled. There was so much to digest of Robert's wicked world, that it took strength to piece together what led to me being raped of my youth.

Grooming leaves you in a confused state of mind, with self-doubt and low self-esteem, swamped with guilt and with a deep distrust of people. Although it took many years to let my defences down and explore this most traumatic time in my life, I was ready when I made the choice to embrace it. In order to begin to do this, I needed to understand that what I had experienced was grooming, so I could heal from the sexual assaults and the psychological torment I had suppressed.

Linking the pieces showed me that, no matter how young you are, you know when something isn't quite right. And these first instincts are what we need to nurture when they arise. However, my adolescent self wasn't taught to question my curiosity and act upon it; I came from an era of 'children must be seen and not heard'. If this negative idea is what we have received from others, then what are we teaching our children today? Are we carrying on reinforcing the same concept and then handing it down to our children, so they don't speak out?

One of the main points in this book was the loss of my voice, and – now that I've found it – I urge others to not allow theirs to become lost in an inner world. Your voice is one of the most powerful tools you have, but only if you train yourself to use it wisely. On the following pages, I've described the links I made from living in a world of grooming and the unfolding revelations of my experience.

Curiosity

We're born curious creatures, though some more than others.

The modelling industry supplied Robert with an endless stream of attractive young girls, and the draped curtain was the main thing that provided a link to reveal the dark world Robert lived in. He used the modelling agency as a front through which he artfully chose his prey to groom, then made sure he gradually won our confidence.

The air grill was the second item that I became curious about when Gina weighed us in the back room, and it became clear why she told us to take everything off and slip the towel round us. The curtain provided Robert with the private space to capture on camera the girls undressing in the changing room; he stood in front of the air grill, filming and taking still shots. This voyeurism began his perverted lust and his fantasising about the girls he would choose to groom.

False Sense of Security

Once Robert had decided to target his favourites, he needed

to lead them and their parents into a false sense of security from the fact that he was both a respectable member of society and someone of value in their daughter's life. As an innocent, trusting teenager, I took Robert's touching as normal behaviour and not the beginning of being primed. This friendliness links with the early phases of grooming.

Robert used charm and flattery to begin a friendship built on deceitful trust, with the help of his girlfriend, to make us feel safe and to fulfil our growing emotional needs. Robert was in no rush; he was a professional at manipulation and controlling naive girls, which would eventually lead to satisfying his obsession for seducing teenage virgins after their 16th birthdays.

Luring Aspiring Beauties

This phase links to maintaining and deepening trust, which is the central role of the grooming process. When Robert felt confident, he lured aspiring young beauties into his home every weekend. These friendships secured a group bond, and our parents were reassured by his girlfriend that this was all part of the modelling training for those with the most potential of becoming successful models. Once he had us in his home, he could exploit our trust, build on the relationship we formed with them and use the friendship to his advantage.

They gave out 'vitamins', and told us they were various multivitamins and good for our health. However, during the investigations the detectives had a theory that these were actually drugs, which was later confirmed by one of the girls, as it was reported that they were tranquillisers and amphetamines. This confirmed my own suspicions that the alcohol Robert gave me was spiked to make me dazed and less inhibited when I was alone with Gina.

Night-time Monster

The 'night-time monster' is a description that links to the years of grooming and the power imbalance in the relationship the abusers had with their victims. We believed and did anything they told us, not realising it was inappropriate to forbid us to wear knickers in bed – they had even added it was disgusting and unhygienic to do so, to make his demands seem normal. This shameless monster wanted us in bed without underwear so he could secretly take pictures while we slept deeply from the tranquillisers they gave us, which they had dubbed 'vitamins'. This made sure we didn't wake up when he pulled back the covers, and manipulated our bodies for his sordid shots to add to his collection from the past 20 years.

The more time we spent with them, the more he gained power to isolate us from our friends and families. They groomed us with attentiveness and generosity by tempting us with living the glamorous high life and introducing us to Robert's wealthy friends, so they too could be supplied with young girls. As we approached the age of consent, Robert blurred the boundaries further by making sexual comments about our ages to prepare us for sexual violation. When it reached the stage of violation, we had become so brainwashed that we didn't see the sexual assaults as rape.

What Lies Behind the Curtain

Behind the curtain stood the dominant figure, who was controlling the situations. Many sexual encounters were filmed at the modelling agency or at his home, featuring him and Gina, other girls and businessmen, plus the tape my parents watched of me vomiting. This explained why he was so angry on this night, because he couldn't use the video to blackmail me if he needed to in the future. He tried to soften this blow with a confession about protecting Gina.

Following this, the police satisfied my curiosity when I wondered what Robert was doing while I remained frozen in bed on the morning the police broke into the house. They found Robert halfway into the loft, frantically trying to conceal pornographic videos showing hundreds of girls undressing or taking part in sex.

As much as it was painful to reflect on the years of grooming, it was liberating to understand Robert's manipulative behaviour, which – in turn – stopped me from blaming myself for something that was out of my control. It's sometimes the most difficult experiences we've endured that show us our purpose in life. Dissecting these revelations and allowing myself to feel the repressed emotions attached to them was the best gift I could give myself, because I gained the courage to speak, to challenge who I wanted to become and to see myself in a different light.

The Healing Process

You have a choice to stand tall and face traumas, yet I know how difficult it is to finally look in the mirror, and look beyond the guilt and shameful fear of judgements from others. Shame is the hardest wound to overcome, since we'll carry this through to other relationships that could become abusive, because we feel unworthy, unacceptable and unlovable. These emotions do dissipate as you process what you've experienced, and you can tell yourself that it wasn't your fault and you aren't to blame for someone else's misdemeanours. When you believe this, you allow yourself to attract more supportive relationships into your life.

Reflecting on and finding meaning from my experience has

brought a sense of clarity and given me the strength to stand up to anything life throws at me. Something that broke me has driven me to be of service to others and to want to share my story about the detrimental effects of grooming. Everyone is different when it comes to the healing process and challenging oneself to make changes in life for the better. I believe that, with the right help, we can be guided to reach a state of contentment, even if the beginning or part of our journey was traumatic. In my personal therapy, I was able to become vulnerable, and to see and hear myself clearly. Even though I felt exposed, it has been the most profound journey. If we can take a leap into unknown territory, the defences we formed will start to break down and we'll become more like ourselves.

We all deserve to have someone to reach out to in our darkest of times, and to have our core needs fulfilled by being accepted and loved for who we are. But, most of all, we need to nurture and be compassionate with ourselves, for this brings change and the wisdom to use our trauma to our advantage. This can take years, so be kind and patient with yourself. If this book can touch just a few people, then it's a job well done in planting seeds for my readers to grow in a new direction and in raising awareness to deter young girls from getting tangled in a web of control from people who are in a far more powerful position than the girls themselves. However, if you've already suffered at the hands of sex offenders, then I hope that reading this book has in some way helped you on your journey towards healing. Stepping inside yourself to find inner peace will be the beginning of you living your life with more freedom.

***

To end this book, I'll share a conversation I had with my parents in the January before I published this book. For the healing journey to come full circle, I had to mend the old rupture between us, tell them I had written a book and tell them the reason why I wanted to share my experience. It took years to process what happened, and I know if I hadn't followed the path of counselling, I wouldn't have been able to have one of my most important conversations with them. In my opinion, to approach one's parents about an experience that affected us all is one of the hardest things to do. However, it's even harder to live with the regret of unspoken words.

As I faced my parents at the dinner table, as I was building up the courage to broach the subject, my chest was thumping.

The only other time I had felt like this was eight years ago on my second day of college. We were instructed to complete a heraldry-based team building exercise.

After presenting our heraldic shields, the tutor asked, 'Does anyone have anything else to add?'

Silence filled the room, and my heart thumped as I thought that my teacher must know there were other things that lay beneath the surface of the idyllic shields we created. Life isn't always a bed of roses, and her words triggered a force that would be able to unlock the chapter I had closed 25 years ago. I knew that if I didn't speak up at that time, then I never would.

This experience allowed me to have a frank conversation with my parents, in which each of us was heard and understood, as we talked about our thoughts and feelings that were stored in the deepest parts of our minds. For me to have my parents' attention and also to listen to them was a powerful moment. I spoke about the guilt and shame I held, the 17-year-old I hated for the pain I'd caused, and how I was sorry. It was such a relief to hear my father say that I had nothing to be sorry for, and they felt guilty and sorry for not knowing what was going on, because they had been hoodwinked. Sitting there and riding the initial uncomfortable wave with my parents deepened our connection and strengthened the relationship I had with my parents as an adult child. This, in a nutshell, is the gift of therapy working at its best.

Grooming Models

The following describes various grooming models, which will help you identify the model used by abusers on you or your child. This information is sourced from Alex Bateman's (2016) safeguarding page at the Virtual College, unless stated otherwise.

The Relationship Model

The relationship model, also referred to as the boyfriend model, is viewed as the most typical method of grooming. This model leads the young person to believe they're in a loving and supportive relationship with another person, but they're unaware they're being coerced into having sex with them and/or others in the abuser's inner circle. There are cases where the relationship model of grooming occurs among peers, sometimes through gang activity. It isn't always girls who are the victims in this scenario either, so the name boyfriend model can be confusing.

The Inappropriate Relationship Model

The inappropriate relationship model of child grooming involves the abuser having an inappropriate amount of power or control over the young person, because of their position in society and/or there being a significant age gap between them. The young person again feels they're in a loving relationship because they're showered with attention, advice, understanding and gifts, and taken on outings.

The Trafficking Model

In this model, young people become victims of the buying and selling of sexual services, and have usually become reliant on the abuser to get their basic needs met. They can be either trafficked within their own country or internationally. The children are passed through networks of perpetrators across towns and cities, where they're forced into sexual activities with multiple abusers. Some young people involved in the organisation of the trafficking process may be used as 'agents' to recruit others into the network, which continues to repeat the vicious cycle of abuse.

The Party Lifestyle Model

This model involves young people being groomed in a group, which gives a feeling of security because of the belief that there's safety in numbers. They're invited to many parties, and are given drugs and alcohol as an incentive to attend more parties, all the while being unaware that the abuser wants repayment in the form of sexual activity. When the child is asked for repayment for the fun they're having, they feel obliged because they do not want to be left out of the group or they feel too scared to say no, which is something the abusers take advantage of.

The next section of this book serves to highlight points from my story about staying safe, the children who are most at risk, signs of grooming and what we can do as parents to keep our children safe. Marilyn Hawes (2012) writes extensively about identifying and managing the issues created by grooming in her handbook *Enough Abuse*.

If you think you're a victim of grooming

Who to Turn To

If you believe you or your child is a victim of grooming, please get in touch with one of the following:

- Parent or caregiver
- Friends
- Teacher
- School counsellor
- Appropriate organisation (listed in the Where to Get Help section on pages 262-3)
- Social services
- Police

What to Look for in Yourself and the Abusive Adult

Please be aware of and question the following behaviours in adults to help you identify potential abuse. Please also note that women can be groomers too, so the following list doesn't just apply to men:

- Disguised sexual comments and compliments from someone significantly older than you.
- An adult shows semi-nudity in front you that makes you feel uncomfortable.
- An adult shows you pornographic material.

- An adult asks you to send nude pictures of yourself to them (or someone else).
- An adult who isn't your parent or guardian controls who you see and what you do.
- An adult confuses you about who you are.
- An adult asks for intimate information about boyfriends and any sexual activity you may have experienced with others.
- An adult makes you take part in sexual acts you haven't discussed and consented to.
- Be alarmed if an adult creates situations to be alone with you.
- Be alarmed if an adult introduces you to a circle of older people, and plies you with treats and alcohol.
- An adult who isn't your parent or guardian keeps tabs on where you are if you're not in their company.
- An adult uses aggression and violence to intimidate you.
- An adult who is exhibiting any of the other behaviours in this list who is also grooming your parents/guardians by showering them with kind gestures.

If you think you're perhaps being groomed, please do the following:

- Trust your initial instincts in noting odd things and strange behaviours.
- Listen to your growing inner voice and act on curiosity.
- Leave any situation when you know something isn't right.
- Talk to a safe person if someone touches you inappropriately and makes you do things you do not want to do.

- Do not take alcohol you haven't seen poured in front of you.
- Talk to others in the group if you're being groomed in a group.

Everyone has a unique story; what one person deems safe may not be safe for another. Grooming affects your ability to respond to your gut instinct because the abuser has used power to control your mind for their purposes. If you're able to remove yourself and seek help from the right people, then you'll save yourself from any more abuse, get yourself on the road to recovery and receive the support you deserve.

What Puts a Child Most at Risk?

The following are situations in which a child will be most at risk of attracting the attention of a groomer:

- **Being too trusting:** A child who has been raised not to doubt its elders and to always look up to them with respect gives the groomer a feeling of superiority that allows them to take advantage of the minor's innocence.
- **An unstable family home environment or being in care:** Children living in these environments are more vulnerable to being taken advantage of because they're seeking stability, secure boundaries, support and love in the outside world.
- **A lack of being nurtured and low self-esteem:** We're only human and seek out relationships to meet our growing needs. We attract people to meet these needs (both consciously and subconsciously), even if it's to our own detriment. Groomers pay attention to this knowledge.
- **Bereavement:** Losing someone of significance can lead

some people to rely on outside affection and to look for someone to talk to if they can't approach anyone in their family. Again, groomers are skilled in showing this support, which draws the abused closer.

- **Previous abuse:** The sex offender will have probed into the background of his/her victim. The abused may lack self-worth because of previous abuse, which makes them an easy target to groom. They may not have experienced secure attachments to others, which the groomer homes in on, making the abused think they're in a loving relationship because they're listened to and understood.

Please be aware that, in my experience, your child won't disclose anything that's happening to them; they'll be confused, feel deeply ashamed and may even love their abuser. As a parent, we need to stay vigilant and in tune when it comes to our children and other young people in our environment. In doing so, we protect them, and make it difficult for predators to gain control and abuse our children. We must be available to our children emotionally and physically, and give as much time to them as possible.

The Signs of Grooming

Many caregivers won't see the things listed in this section as signs of grooming, but will instead regard them as common teenage behaviours, so by no means jump to conclusions that your child is in danger if they display one of these. However, I'd show concern if you see more than four of the things listed here and intervene before any harm occurs:

- Your child is secretive about who they're with and what they're doing.

- Your child has any associations with significantly older people.
- One or more adults are paying too much attention to your child.
- One or more adults, whom you've never met, are involved with your child.
- Your child becomes associated with new peer groups / a gang.
- Your child stays away from home for long periods.
- The relationship with your child has dramatically changed; e.g. they aren't relating with you on a deeper level.
- Your child isn't hanging out with old school friends.
- Your child is stealing – this could be acting out for attention and may be a cry for help.
- Your child has new possessions that you haven't bought for them, such as clothes, jewellery, mobile phones and extra money.
- Your child has changed aspects of her/his appearance, such as their hair, the amount/type of make-up worn and/or wearing revealing clothes.
- Your child has changed her/his behaviour, mannerisms and temperament, such as having mood swings, being aggressive or showing sexual behaviour.
- Your child is using drugs and alcohol.
- Your child is self-harming/depressed.
- Your child is promiscuous.
- Your child is pregnant.

How to Keep Your Children Safe from Predators

The following actions can help to keep your child safe from predators:

- Pay attention to your child's emotional needs.
- Tune in and listen to your child.
- Communicate with your child's growing adult self.
- Don't be an overpowering parent; be your child's friend as well as their parent.
- Question anything that seems odd in your child's behaviour.
- Teach your child about protecting their personal space.
- Teach your child that certain touching is not OK, and it's OK if they don't want to hug family members or friends.
- Teach your child it isn't OK to accept alcohol and cigarettes off significantly older people.
- Talk to your child about autonomy and how it can be lost.
- If your child has the courage to speak to you about abuse, believe them.
- If your child has been groomed, help them to understand what is going on if they don't see they were groomed.
- Act straight away, and contact the police or social services.

The impact of grooming is immense, which is why it's important to encourage support through therapy or seek survivor groups. In my experience, this should be sooner rather than later, so the healing process can begin and they can start to deal with the psychological trauma. As a parent, I can only imagine what it's like to live with knowing your child was groomed and you weren't able to protect them. It's a distressing time for everyone, and each person needs to be heard and understood, so it's helpful for parents to seek a therapist too, to manage their overwhelming emotions. Therapy supports your mental health and builds your confidence to mend the ruptures in family relationships.

WHERE TO GET HELP

NSPCC

Helpline: 0808 800 5000 (24/7 service)

https://nspcc.org.uk/

This is the UK's leading charity specialising in child protection and the prevention of cruelty to children. The helpline is free, and is for anyone – children or adults – who is concerned about a child at risk of abuse.

Rape Crisis

Helpline: 0808 802 9999 (12pm–2.30pm and 7pm–9.30pm)

https://rapecrisis.org.uk/

Rape Crisis offers support and counselling for those affected by rape and sexual abuse.

Victim Support

Helpline: 0808 168 9111

https://www.victimsupport.org.uk/

Victim Support offers free, confidential support for anyone who has been raped or sexually assaulted, now or in the past.

Rape and Sexual Abuse Support Centre (RASAC)

National Helpline: 0808 802 9999 (12pm–2.30pm and 7pm–9.30pm)

https://rasasc.org.uk/

This national helpline provides emotional and practical support for survivors of rape and childhood sexual abuse, and for their families and friends.

The Survivors Trust

Helpline: 0808 801 0818

thesurvivorstrust.org

The Survivors Trust aims to support and empower survivors of rape, sexual violence and /or childhood sexual abuse, through providing a collective voice and peer networking for members. It raises awareness about sexual abuse and/or rape, and its effects on survivors, their supporters and society at large. It informs of and acknowledges effective responses to rape and sexual abuse on a local, regional and national level.

Freedom from Abuse

07484541727

marilyn.hawes@freedom-abuse.org

freedom-abuse.org

Freedom from Abuse not only teaches parents and carers how to protect their children from sexual abuse, but also teaches how to prevent it happening.

Childline

Helpline: 0800 1111

https://www.childline.org.uk/

Childline provides a free, private and confidential service. Whatever you're worried about, no matter how big or small it seems, and whenever you need help, they're there for you online and/or on the phone, anytime.

REFERENCES

Bateman, A. (2016). *What Are The Different Grooming Models?* [online] Virtual College. Available at: https://www.virtual-college.co.uk/news/safeguarding/2018/01/different-grooming-models [Accessed 14 December 2018], p.202.

Hawes, M. (2012). *Enough Abuse.* [online] Available at: https://www3.havering.gov.uk/Documents/Care-for-adults-and-children/Sexual-Exploitation/NSPCC-Parents-Advice-Booklet.pdf [Accessed 20 December 2018].

ACKNOWLEDGEMENTS

Where do I begin to thank all those who have been involved in my journey so far, when there are so many people who have touched my life in many different ways? I've come to realise that it's sometimes the most painful of relationships that have had the most impact and driven me to where I am today. So, I'll be eternally grateful for my path crossing with the paths of these people, and that they've taught me something new about myself.

First of all, I want to start by thanking my precious daughter. You've had the most positive impact on my life because without you I'd be wandering around the world trying to find myself in different cities that wouldn't have the answers. You became my anchor that settled me in one city, and helped me to begin an inward journey to find myself and gain wisdom about the person I've become.

I thank my wonderful parents for your constant love and support when I've felt broken. You've given me the core necessities of what it is to be a good person with morals, manners, respect and family values. I count myself lucky to be part of a large family that keeps my life full of vibrancy and keeps me grounded, so I don't forget where I came from. I adore each and every one of you.

To Georgie, thank you for being a constant rock through my highs and lows, and pushing me to publish this book, because you want to read it! You're the kindest and most generous person I know, and a true diamond.

To my confidant, Chris, for inspiring and encouraging me to revisit my memoirs and bring this book to life, I thank you.

To my book coach, Alexa, thank you for your guidance and brainstorming phone calls. You kept me focused and on my toes with homework every month, and the question 'What is the point I'm making?' swirled round my head as I wrote. And for your reassurance that it was normal to wonder what the hell I was doing, when I had wobbly moments about exposing myself in a sensitive subject, I thank you. To my editor Lindsay, for your sensitive approach towards my book and tweaks to help my words bounce off the pages, you are great at what you do. Thank you.

To all my friends, and those of you who have influenced my thinking and made me realise that – with thought and effort – anything is possible, I thank you.

ABOUT THE AUTHOR

Claire Gray was born and raised in Manchester, England. She left school in 1993 at age 16, and travelled to Asia for modelling contracts before settling in London when her daughter was born in 2007. Claire qualified as a counsellor in spring 2017 and received an advanced diploma in humanistic integrative counselling; this experience was the most terrifying and exciting time in her life, apart from giving birth!

In 2018, Claire completed a foundation course at The Institute of Psychoanalysis to deepen her understanding of the unconscious mind and the process of repression. These achievements have taught her many things about who she is. Claire found herself on an inward journey, she believes we are all unique beings with a purpose in life, however, finding this purpose can be a struggle. Claire began to find meaning from her experiences and now, 25 years on, her purpose and calling was to publish her personal memoir to raise awareness and help people during these traumatic times. Claire currently volunteers at a bereavement service, where she helps her clients work through the stages of grief in a safe, nurturing environment. She is passionate about this work and is forever fascinated with the therapeutic alliance, because she always discovers something new about herself when serving as a source of light to others. A tutor once told her, 'You get the clients you need'; this means that the people who cross your path are there to awaken you and help you grow.